The Outdoor Classroom in Practice, Ages 3–7

The outdoor environment is now an integral part of many early years settings and schools, but is it being used to its full potential?

Providing extensive, challenging and ever-changing outdoor play experiences is an essential and valuable aspect of early years education. This book offers comprehensive guidance on how the outdoor environment can be used to teach and challenge all children across a range of settings drawing on forest school practice.

Following a month-by-month format, each chapter provides a selection of theme-related play experiences alongside planning and evaluations of how the ideas described were carried out, and reveals the impact that they had on the children. Including detailed information on the role of the adult, the environment, planning and using children's interests to guide their learning and development, the book features:

- over 100 full-colour photographs to illustrate practice
- diary entries that reflect how the planning was delivered, what changes were made and how aspects of learning were recorded and assessed
- examples of practice as well as comprehensive resource lists and safety guidelines
- links to indoor play and opportunities at home.

Written by a leading authority on forest school practice and full of practical ideas that can be adapted to suit individual children's needs, this book aims to inspire practitioners to make the most of the outdoor environment throughout the year.

Karen Constable is an experienced early years teacher, having worked for almost twenty years in nursery and school settings. Specialising in how children learn, and using the outdoor environment, Karen has worked across schools in Somerset supporting teachers and students to improve children's learning. She is currently a reception class teacher and early years leader, working with children ranging from two to five years at Mark First School, UK.

Sandy Green worked within the early years sector for over thirty-five years, initially as a nursery nurse in both education and social services settings and later as a lecturer in further education. She is now an educational consultant and has written extensively on early years education.

The Outdoor Classroom in Practice, Ages 3–7

A month-by-month guide to forest school provision

Karen Constable

Edited by Sandy Green

Routledge
Taylor & Francis Group

LONDON AND NEW YORK

First published 2015
by Routledge
2 Park Square, Milton Park, Abingdon, Oxon OX14 4RN

and by Routledge
711 Third Avenue, New York, NY 10017

Routledge is an imprint of the Taylor & Francis Group, an informa business

British Library Cataloguing in Publication Data
A catalogue record for this book is available from the British Library

Library of Congress Cataloging in Publication Data
Constable, Karen.
The outdoor classroom in practice, ages 3-7 : a month-by-month guide to forest school provision / Karen Constable.
pages cm
1. Outdoor education. 2. Early childhood education. I. Title.
LB1047.C734 2015
371.3'84—dc23
2014025291

ISBN: 978-1-138-83150-6 (hbk)
ISBN: 978-0-415-72905-5 (pbk)
ISBN: 978-1-315-85134-1 (ebk)

Typeset in Bembo and Frutiger
by FiSH Books Ltd, Enfield

Contents

Preface

I was asked recently what my motivation was for teaching and writing about outdoor learning. Initially I was a bit baffled; why would you not be motivated by nature's diversity? It was clear to me why I do this, why I am driven to share my passion. Shouldn't we all be aware of the benefits of being outdoors, learning new skills, sharing play with friends and enjoying our ever-changing world? Is that just for children, or can't adults gain from it as well?

Over the years I have worked with young children I have come to learn a lot about how they learn, the impact others can have on that learning, both positive and negative and the necessity of allowing children to be children.

When I was offered the opportunity to train as a Forest School Leader, the course was in its first year and was under-subscribed. I jumped at the chance to explore and learn about a new area of children's learning. I wasn't disappointed. From the outset it was clear that this new style of learning was going to have a huge impact on early years provision.

Over the weeks of learning and working at Forest School with Bridgwater College, I learnt about self-esteem and confidence in a way that it had never been presented to me before. I learnt about using tools, keeping children safe, managing, but not removing risk. I created a bank of ideas and activities, all of which I tried out myself before taking them to the children. I took my own children out with fresh eyes, building dens, lighting fires, sawing logs and we learnt together. My own confidence grew; I felt good about my achievements and most crucially I had immense fun. If learning outdoors could have that impact on me, imagine what it could do for the children I worked with.

My life is embedded in the outdoors, both in my work and at home. Being outside I feel alive, aware of my world, in tune with the weather and the seasons. I understand the impact our over-populated world is having and strive to reduce my own 'footprint'. Again, if I feel like this, won't the children?

I truly believe that everyone has some connection with the environment, even the most reluctant non-believer must surely feel something when they notice the frequent seasonal changes around them?

I am motivated by the ever-changing beauty, the life-cycles of the trees I pass on the way to work, the stillness of the river I stop and admire each morning. I am driven to share all this and more with my class in the hope that some of these young children will grow up acknowledging that the world is amazing; that they can recognise how they can be a part of it; that they can gain peace and calm in the tranquillity. I want them to begin to understand that somewhere in their busy, noisy lives they can be themselves, be independent and happy, be a part of something that is bigger than their everyday normality.

If just one or two of my children gain an affinity with their world then I have done my part to ensure that our world will remain as beautiful as it is now. The next generation are in charge of their own future, but if we don't teach them about it, how will they know?

What greater motivation is there than that?

Acknowledgements

The author and publishers would like to thank the following for their cooperation and support during the process of publishing this book.

The staff, children and parents at Mark Church of England First School and Mark Harvest Pre-school for their support and encouragement throughout the process and for the use of their ideas and photos and their permission to include them in the book.
My family and friends for their continuing support and encouragement.
To Sandy, for encouraging me to keep going and ensuring this book was finished.

Introduction

The term forest school is now commonplace across early years settings and schools in both the UK and further afield. From its early UK beginnings in a Somerset college it has grown into a nationwide provision for children and students in all areas of education. Qualifications are offered by various providers to instil skills and confidence into the workforce and an increasing number of diverse settings are now looking at how forest school can enhance the provision they offer. Forest schools are running in rural and urban areas with equal success, and what was once a rather daunting prospect for parents is now far more accepted, with fewer obvious concerns and anxieties.

The opportunity to take children out of classrooms and cosy nurseries has captured the creative imaginations of many practitioners and with the benefits so clearly visible it has become an integral part of the curriculum, with requirements for outdoor play now taking a higher place in the statutory education of children with the foundation stage.

How each setting has interpreted the need for outdoor provision is down to the individual establishments and forest school can now be seen taking place in many different ways. Each setting that embraces forest school has taken the time to make sure it suits their own individual needs and each experience is different to another. This uniqueness is creating exciting and wide-ranging experiences for children from many backgrounds and is without doubt offering opportunities that were otherwise beginning to be phased out of children's lives.

As children growing up in the 1960s and 1970s we were able to roam freely, uninhibited by parental fears and media interferences. The days of taking your bike off with a group of friends to make dens and build hideaways and returning in time for tea are all but over for children of the twenty-first century. Media interpretation of risk and injury has led to a culture of over-protective and insecure parenting, stifling the freedom that is so important for young children.

In their home environment there is little chance the children will take a risk and learn from their mistakes through trial and error. Even in public play areas the surfaces are safe to prevent injury, the height of play structures is reduced and parents are encouraged to supervise their children at all times. Children are having their experiences managed, their time is filled with supervised experiences and outdoor play is often restricted by adverse weather.

The forest school movement is changing people's perceptions of some of these aspects. It is teaching children and their parents that taking a risk is OK, getting it wrong is OK and learning from your mistakes is vital. A child who has never got stuck part way up a tree will never know how to overcome their fear. If they have never stung themselves in a nettle bed, they will never know that the stinging lasts for such a short time. They will not know how to look after themselves and their friends if someone is always doing the looking after for them.

There is clear alarm among educationalists worldwide that children are losing touch with their natural environment and that they do not know about the impact humans are having on the area we live in. These children are the same people, who in thirty years' time will be expected to solve the problems associated with global warming, an increasing population, a housing shortage and a diminishing supply of natural energy. If we are to create a population with an infinity with their own world, then we have to steer it in the right direction. Allowing children to become at one with their own natural space is crucial if we are to retain the countryside in a form that we will recognise. Creating a love of the outdoors can only be done when children are exposed to it in reality. Forest schools are setting out to change the outlook of a generation of children.

Forest school seeks to reintroduce some of the elements of play that are lacking. Through gentle introduction the children begin to learn how to look after themselves, how to look out for their friends and how to change their approach to ensure their own safety.

Different settings will apply their own rules and will have their own method of introducing the children, but generally the expected outcome remains the same: that the children should be happy, independent, have high self-esteem and confidence is the desired benefit we are all seeking.

With well-prepared staff, inspired opportunities, a degree of freedom and a high rate of success, children accessing forest school will be happy and able. They will be learning transferable life skills and will know and love their environment. They might not be skills that the children recognise or understand themselves, but they are clearly visible throughout educational settings where this style of learning is readily and frequently available.

This book sets out to demonstrate how a forest school-style learning experience can be introduced and used in an ordinary educational environment. The setting is a school with an integrated pre-school and the sessions have been planned and delivered for children from the ages of three to six. Each chapter sets out to provide ideas for the sessions, using each month of the year to demonstrate how the environment and weather can play such a crucial part in the child's experiences. Each series of activities can be delivered in the order written or as one-off sessions. They can be used in the month suggested or in some cases repeated throughout the year. As with all early years experiences they will need to be adjusted to suit your other planning and the needs of your specific group of children. There is some reference to specific items discussed in previous months.

The opening of each chapter includes a look at one aspect of the forest school provision, covering such areas as managing the site, preparing the resources, working with parents and making assessments. It is difficult to show chronologically how you should carry out these suggestions, but by the end of your year you will have considered the most important factors of your forest school provision.

Every month there is a case study that shows how learning can be interpreted and used for the child's progression, either in that session or in follow-up opportunities. The teacher blog is a candid look at what actually took place. As all practitioners are fully aware, no amount of planning can cover every eventuality and with such a fluid approach to learning, forest school often presents learning opportunities that were not planned or expected.

1 September

Preparing for forest school

For many settings, September is the beginning of a new year, with a change of children, parents and possibly some staff members. It is a time to ensure that your practice is planned, risk assessed and prepared for the new term.

The most important resource you are going to need in your forest school is the kit bag. This piece of equipment will go with you on every session, carrying essential resources and emergency aids. Some items you will use frequently, others will rarely or never come out of the bag but still need to be there. This bag needs replenishing and checking after every visit and will then be ready to be used by others, in the knowledge they too will have everything they need.

The forest school kit bag

- First-aid kit
- Emergency procedures documents
- Medical information for each individual and emergency contact details for each member of the group
- Risk assessments
- Mobile phone, fully charged
- Clean water
- Accident forms
- Medication for individuals
- Wet wipes, hand gel
- Nappy sacks and toileting things
- Suncream
- Spare clothing
- Thermos of hot water
- Chocolate/sugary food
- Plastic bag
- Roll mat and blanket
- Fire blanket
- Bucket of water
- Burns kit
- Bivi Bag

Some of these items may not need to be carried on your person. Take into account the setting's proximity to your forest area when making this decision. Perhaps some of the kit can be kept and maintained in the resource storage in forest area? If this is your preferred method of ensuring safety is maintained make sure the storage is unlocked and, if necessary, the kit is taken to the area in which you are working. You might have all paperwork in the setting, this helps to make medical details and contact details safer and readily available at all times. Using a mobile phone would ensure a quick response back at the base. Just a word of caution: make sure your mobile network coverage is adequate for calling. If not, consider using a two way radio instead.

You will also need a first-aid kit. This may be kept in the site or added to the kit bag. Whichever you decide is the most practical for you, it is essential that it is maintained. Choosing one member of staff, with the appropriate first-aid certificate to be responsible for this usually works well. Maintaining dated and signed records means that others can take over if necessary.

Your first-aid kit

- Latex gloves
- Bandages
- Plasters
- Burns gel
- Burn dressing
- Dressings
- Eye wash
- Scissors
- Cotton wool
- Antiseptic wipes
- Tick removers
- Sterile water
- Cling film
- Bites and stings cream or spray (parental permission required)
- Cool packs

TO DO

- Ensure all parents have given written consent for their children to attend forest school.
- Send out clothing lists.
- Plan and deliver workshops for parents and children.
- Set up your forest school kit bag and first-aid kit.
- Update staff on any changes since the previous visits.
- Check your forest area. Look for any evidence of trespassers, danger caused by fallen branches or damaged boundaries.
- Replenish your forest school resources.
- Set up your observation and assessment procedures.

September at forest school

This is the month of transitions and new beginnings for many of your children. Much of your work in forest school will be settling in and reassuring the more wary members of your group. Consider whether the children need to have their key worker present for some of their early visits and wherever possible make sure they visit with a friend in their group. Keeping these early sessions shorter also reduces anxiety for new children.

Setting up opportunities for parents to visit will remove some of their anxiety, but within this consider how the child will behave if their parent comes too. You don't want to set a precedent that the child believes that a parent will always be there. If you feel this is a consideration in your group, perhaps you could arrange for parents to visit with a different group of children? Alternatively set up a forest school 'fun session' just for parents. This usually gets more dads involved than you might expect at other events, so is a good way to get to know more about the child's family life.

Invest time now in settling in and instilling the forest school rules and you will hopefully eliminate problems further down the line.

Keep the rules very simple for the children and send the rules home for the parents to reinforce as well.

Rules

- Don't go in or out of the area without a grown up.
- Keep out of the log circle area.
- Don't climb the gates or fences.
- Respect the plants and animals that live in our forest area.
- Don't pick up a stick longer than your arm.
- Look after your friends.
- Have fun and enjoy your visit.

Finding our way around

Objectives

- To explore using the senses of sight, sound, touch and hearing.
- To find natural objects that provoke curiosity.
- To share excitement with others.

Adult initiated ideas

Give the children the entire session to explore their new environment, looking for special places and natural curiosities. Some children will want to be with an adult in these early stages, others will be far more confident. To ensure you feel comfortable, make sure you set the ground rules. If you want the children to stay within sight of you, make sure they know. Even with this rule you may want to make sure that children are shadowed to maintain their safety.

During the snack time initiate a conversation about what the children have been doing. Make some notes of the specific things they have enjoyed, you can then provide more individual opportunities in the future.

Take photos to share in the setting, add to the website or send home to reassure parents.

The children finding their way back to the log circle.

The more confident children wanted to run around the paths they found.

The more cautious children stayed with a friend.

Hide and seek

Objectives

- To explore with confidence.
- To find out how to keep themselves safe at forest school.
- To work as part of a small group to achieve a goal.

Adult initiated ideas

This activity was introduced in the early days of forest school at Bridgwater College to help the children become familiar with their surroundings and to provide them with a mechanism for getting some help if they needed it.

Split the group into two and send half away to hide in a group together. The first group calls out, '1, 2, 3, where are you?' The hiding group returns the call with, '1, 2, 3 we're over here!' Working as a group, the finders try to locate the hiding group. The calls are repeated several times until the children are all back together. As the children get more confident with this game over the next few weeks, the hiding group could split up and use several locations.

Explain to the children that they can use this call any time they need to find an adult in the outdoor area. It's also a good idea to share this with parents so that they understand what the children have learnt.

Some of the paths are a bit daunting when the undergrowth is in full leaf, but it does make great hiding places.

Looking for somewhere to hide.

This boy was happy to be left counting while the other children went off to hide.

Exploring independently

> ### Objectives
>
> - To begin to talk about their local environment.
> - To share their own views and opinions in a small group.
> - To explore freely with increasing confidence.

Adult initiated ideas

Send the children off to explore with their friends. Some children may need an adult to go with them, but try to let the children make the decisions about where they go. Encourage the children to explore all the hidden corners and dens. What do they like, or maybe not like, about each place?

Back in the log circle talk about the places the children have found. Are there any places all the children agreed were special? What makes them special?

Discuss how we can keep the place special. Talk about keeping it tidy and clean for us and others to use.

Exploring the dens.

Sharing the new den with friends. Each child has their own view of what the den was.

Becoming more independent and going off alone.

Trying out new activities

Objectives

- To explore some of the resources that are available for them.
- To try a range of activities independently.

Adult initiated ideas

Provide a range of resource boxes for the children to access freely. Ensure there are items that will encourage the children to move around the area independently.

- Den building kit (fabric sheeting, camouflage fabric, tarpaulin, rope, string, pegs)
- Mini-beast hunting kit (magnifying glasses, clear pots, trowels, identification kits)
- Paper, pencils and wax crayons
- Card with double-sided tape, cut into crown and bracelet shapes

Detail the adults with providing support and ideas when asked, without leading more than necessary.

The children enjoyed exploring what they could do with the resource boxes.

These girls worked together successfully to make several bark rubbings.

Child initiated ideas

Much of this month is about introducing the children to their new learning space. Available resources are deliberately limited for the first few weeks to encourage the children to find their own play and experiences.

For these sessions it is suggested that the children are allowed to use the resources that are naturally around them in their play.

The children benefited from the time they had to look around on their own.

RESOURCES

Adult initiated ideas:

- Forest school kit bag
- Forest school drinks bag
- Den building kit
- Mini-beast hunting kit
- Paper, pencils, crayons
- Card, double-sided tape

Child initiated ideas:

- There are few resources required for these sessions because of the nature of the exploration taking place. But if you do want resources available those listed above should be enough to keep children interested for these shorter sessions.

Case study

During our settling in process we had more children than usual who were a little unsure about the freedom offered to them. These children wanted to stay close to the adults, with one girl, Kimberly, needing her hand held throughout each of the first three sessions. None of these children showed any anxiety in the build-up to the forest school sessions, but when offered activities that involved them being independent they were very unsure.

Following a conversation with all staff it was agreed we would maintain this close contact for the less confident children, but would ensure that it was always a different adult that was available. We hoped this would help those children not to become too dependent on one particular person.

By the end of the third session all but one of these children were playing happily, still within sight, but without direct contact with an adult. Kimberly was still hand-holding throughout each session. Following the play that we had observed in the setting we introduced an element of role play into the outdoor area. Bringing with us blankets, cushions and soft toys, the objective was to involve Kimberly in familiar play but in a different space.

The first time we did this she showed no interest in continuing the play we had witnessed inside. But on the second visit Kimberly came to the session with her own small teddy. She told us that she wanted to play with her teddy under a specific tree, but with a particular adult to play with them. Throughout the session she enjoyed building a small bed and a chair for her bear, using sticks and leaves, together with the blankets and cushions. By the end of the session Kimberly hadn't noticed that the adult had withdrawn a short way, but she had embraced the offer from two of the other children to help her.

The next session Kimberly came excited and ready to play again, on this occasion she didn't ask for any adult help. Within a few weeks she was wandering off further and playing more readily with the other children in her group.

Monthly blog

Because our forest school has been up and running for several years we are now seeing the siblings of previous pupils coming into our setting. Generally their confidence in this new play area is higher than it was in the early years and the support we receive from the parents is very positive. Many families come with tales of their previous experiences and often how they have followed that learning as a family outside of forest school.

Because of this independence and confidence we have needed to revise our transition programme, shortening it by several weeks. The result of this is that the children are quicker to get involved in all aspects of outdoor play. The down side is that there are still some children who are very wary and less confident who need to be treated with more caution.

To overcome this we have introduced extra sessions to help the children who need more support. In the autumn term this additional support took place in very small groups and involved a quick walk to the area and a short walk and play, before returning to the setting. We used a camera to take pictures that were printed and displayed inside, and after each visit a photo was chosen by the child to take home and share.

This process took a little more planning than is normally required, but we felt it was worth the effort and certainly the majority of the less confident children soon caught up with their peer group.

2 October

Setting up a forest school environment in your setting

The first and most important aspect of setting up any forest school-style learning is the environment. There is a misconception that forest school needs extensive woodlands and whilst there is no doubt that this would be every practitioners preferred location, for many of us this is not going to be an option. So, before considering where you will carry out these sessions, it may be that you will have to change your thinking about forest school. Consider forest school as a teaching and learning approach, rather than a specific place. Forest school over the years has become more about how children use a unique space to develop social and personal skills, rather than a dedicated trip to local woodlands.

Forest schools have been set up successfully in all manner of spaces; local churchyards, a neighbour's paddock, the corner of the school field and in one case a small courtyard has been happily used for forest school. If you are lucky enough to have trees, an orchard or a wild area on the school grounds then this is ideal. Perhaps you can take children off your site to a nearby location, but this has transport implications, as well as more time restraints. Consider all the options including using several of the above suggestions throughout the year.

The ideal environment provides shelter and secret places to hide.

We enhanced our area and provided additional physical challenge by adding a simple log path.

A neighbouring orchard provides a new outdoor space for an occasional visit.

When you have your location, you should next look into the health and safety necessities. Make sure you take into account any existing policies your setting already abides by and ensure that forest school has a specific policy of its own. What adult ratios are legal for your site, age of children and the activities you will be doing? How will you ensure you always meet them?

Which members of staff will be involved, either each visit or occasionally? Do they need training, off-site certificated training or will you be leading training for the whole staff? Check you have a qualified first-aider in your group. There are specific first-aid courses for people working with children in these environments. Does anyone need to update their certificate? Will you need supportive volunteer parents to ensure ratios are maintained? If so, can they join you for training sessions?

What activities are you likely to be carrying out? If you are new to forest school you are unlikely to be introducing fires and tools immediately. Perhaps you could write an action plan that helps you stay focused on what you will be introducing over the next year?

How often will you be using your forest school area? Is it in close enough proximity for it to be used in a free flow way alongside your current practice? If not, identify regular times when you can take groups of children. If you are in a nursery setting make sure your sessions are planned to allow all your children an opportunity to take part. If you are in a school, do you need to take account of what other classes will be doing? Maybe you can rota the area to give each class a defined session when they know the space can be theirs. If the space is big enough can several groups work outside together?

TO DO

- During this month start to embed forest school into all aspects of your teaching and learning, in particular involving parents. Begin to send home frequent updates to ensure all parents know what their children have been enjoying. This could be in the form of a photo of their child, a picture the child has taken themselves or a brief outline of the sessions' main aims and outcomes.

- Keep your website current, update pictures regularly, ensuring that you have the correct consents to use photos of the children.

- Start a blog page for parents, once again keep it current. Consider allocating this task to a specific staff member and if possible giving them enough time to do it frequently.

- Have you got a display area that the children could be in charge of?

October at forest school

This is the month that sees the most autumn changes in both the environment and the weather and with this, changes to the conditions in which the children are working. The ground is probably going to be muddier than they have been used to, leaves will be falling and once on the ground they quickly become slippery. None of these are hazards that should concern you or the children, but it would be sensible to be mindful of them and be prepared to offer additional support if it is needed.

This set of planning takes advantage of the autumn conditions, using the leaves and seed heads as a learning tool for the children. It is also a lovely way for the children to

A chance to play in the autumn leaves is never missed at this time of year.

notice that their new learning space will be ever changing. Place considerable focus on this aspect of forest school, planning autumn hunts for seeds and colours and showing how the changes are taking place.

If the weather changes suddenly remind everyone to ensure the children are well prepared. It is about this stage in the year that some parents begin to question the wisdom of their child being out in all weathers, so keep the visits frequent and positive.

The children will already be showing signs of increased confidence, remind them about the rules and boundaries frequently to reduce the risk of harm.

Exploring autumn colours

Objectives

- To recognise that there are many shades of one colour.
- To make judgements about the lightness and darkness of the different shades.
- To make independent decisions about the materials they use.
- To enjoy and explore their changing environment.

Adult initiated ideas

The children will have noticed the increasing number of autumn leaves on the ground and with some adult intervention may have talked about why the leaves are changing colour and falling from the trees.

Use these experiences to introduce a leaf collecting activity.

The children can select a colour swatch from the basket and gather a range of leaves that they feel are similar in colour.

Can the children sort their leaves from lightest to darkest?

Give the children a selection of paper and card to choose from. These should already have double-sided tape fixed to them. The children can peel back the protective cover and fix their collection of leaves to the tape.

The children enjoy turning their artwork into autumn crowns or wristbands to wear home afterwards.

Ruby was excited to find feathers and blackberries she could add to her crown of leaves.

Exploring shape and pattern

Objectives

- To look closely at the shapes and patterns of autumn leaves.
- To notice the differences between the leaves in the outdoor area.
- To make independent decisions based on their own ideas.

Adult initiated ideas

Provide the children with some laminated sheets that have leaf outlines on them. Can the children find the leaves that are the same shape? Using identification charts and with an adult to support and read, help the children find out the name of the tree their leaf comes from.

Encourage them to look for several kinds of leaves and the trees they have fallen from. Can they make a picture with their leaves?

Provide paper and wax crayons for the children to use if they want to make wax rubbings of the leaves or tree bark.

Take full advantage of ready-made resources to add to your activities. (www.naturedetectives.org.uk)

Finding out about seeds

Objectives

- To show more confidence in exploring the outdoor area independently.
- To enjoy finding out about their environment through first-hand exploration.
- To show creativity in their approach to a task.

Adult initiated ideas

Explain to the children that many plants die back at this time of year. Do the children know how plants make sure they continue to grow in the future (seeds)? What experiences do the children have of seeds?

Explain that there are many seeds still in the outdoor classroom, have the children seen any?

Send them away to look for dying foliage that contains seed heads. Give the children a small yoghurt pot in which to collect them and a magnifying glass so they can look closely at them.

Provide paper and card, glue and double-sided tape and ask the children to use their seeds to create some art work.

If you wanted this to be a part of a bigger project take a large selection of seeds back to the setting to dry out. These can be used in several ways:

- Make homemade paper that contains the seeds. This paper can be cut up and planted and hopefully some of the seeds will germinate.
- Dry the seeds out and plant early in spring to see what they grow into.
- Add them to the collage area.
- Put them on an autumn display, showing pictures of the plants they came from.

Looking for seeds among the foliage.

Sonnie took his seeds back to the classroom where he turned them into a picture.

The children asked to add some packeted seeds to their pictures.

Inspecting spider webs

> **Objectives**
>
> - To notice some of the everyday elements of the outdoors.
> - To wonder at and question some of nature's work.
> - To recognise some of the skills the creatures around us have.

Adult initiated ideas

Choose a cold morning where the morning dew is still quite heavy. During the autumn months spiders make elaborate and undisturbed webs in all manner of places. Ask the children to search out the most impressive web they can find. They will be more easily discovered with dew on them, but for this activity look for webs to use that are drier.

Spray the web with hairspray and gently sprinkle with talc. Carefully collect the web, from behind, on a piece of black card. It will take the children some time to get the hang of this activity and they will need support, but when collected the webs make a great talking point and show the amazing construction of an everyday occurrence.

To make the webs more interesting spray them with silver or gold paint. Take care not to spray the foliage around the web and ensure there is no spider present.

The finished pictures can be displayed back at the centre and can lead to a topic about spiders and their webs.

Provide lots of rope and string and allow the children to make their own large-scale webs in the outdoor area, using trees and bushes to tie to. Can the children climb through their web, without disturbing it?

Look for spider webs that have a traditional shape and treat them carefully.

Child initiated ideas

This month provide resources to which the children have already been introduced, den building, bug hunting, etc. But also provide one or two new opportunities:

- Rope and string to make stick bundles (the children will need to be shown how to do this initially)
- Paper, pencils and wax crayons
- Collection pots
- Natural materials, some can be brought in to provide some more unusual variations

RESOURCES

Adult initiated ideas:

- Forest school kit bag
- Forest school drinks bag
- Card and paper cut into strips, double-sided tape
- Colour swatches, use autumn colours and greens
- Laminated sheets with leaf outlines, leaf identification charts
- Paper and card, glue, sticky-tape
- Seed collection containers/yoghurt pots, magnifying glasses
- Paper and glue
- Hairspray, talc, spray paints, dark coloured card
- Rope and string

Child initiated ideas:

- Den building box
- Mini-beast hunting kit
- Paper and wax crayons
- Selection of natural materials (shells, stones, pine cones, coconut shells, bark and log slices)

Case study

Billy was a confident four-year-old, who, in the classroom liked to lead the play and often initiated new ideas. He always had a group of children around him and appeared to be a natural leader. At home we understood he spent a lot of time in his extensive garden, exploring and frequently returning inside with a collection of 'treasure' he had gathered.

In the forest school sessions, Billy was quiet and worryingly withdrawn. He didn't show the same confidence and was taking a long time to be independent of the adults. He rarely joined in the other games and allowed his closest friends to run off without him.

We were aware that often the children who showed the most confidence inside were the ones who found outside the hardest to adjust to. But we had made the mistake of believing Billy's home life would counteract that and that he would enjoy his new adventures.

Staff were gentle with Billy coaxing him into games with others and taking time to play with him themselves and over several sessions he became less anxious, but still not the boisterous child we were used to. In our approach we gather as much information as we can from parents to help with this settling in period. In discussion with Billy's Mum we discovered that Billy had a particular pair of boots he liked to wear when he was 'hunting'. We suggested that perhaps these could be brought into school on the days we were going outside.

The next session Billy came to school with his hunting boots and his treasure box. He was a different child on that occasion and once again Billy was surrounded by his friends, sharing his treasure and suggesting they went looking for some more.

Throughout the session Billy and his friends gathered small items to add to the box, all of which he was excited to take home at the end of the day. Billy continued to wear his hunting boots and collect treasure for several more sessions, but on each visit we noticed that he spent less time treasure hunting and more time trying out other activities.

After just six visits Billy left his treasure basket at the log circle and only picked it up again at the end of the session. When his Mum next went shopping she brought him another pair of hunting boots just to keep at school.

Monthly blog

We try hard to find new ideas to bring into forest school and one of these was the activity with the spider's webs. We had seen the results but never tried it ourselves. Believing it to be quite easy we first experimented with the children in tow. They were excited and rather over anxious to catch a web. In their enthusiasm and our inexperience we demolished several webs without any success. The children were heavy-handed in collecting the webs and several beautiful webs turned into sticky lumps on the card before we achieved any success.

Keeping the children interested when activities don't go to plan can be challenging, so we gave them a challenge of using the rope to build their own webs while we practised 'catching' the webs. Without the children jostling around several webs were successfully transferred to card.

The children were called back to look and then sent away to find their own webs. With fewer children around and more time to be careful staff were able to make several successful pictures that were returned to the classroom for examination.

It still turned into an activity that was far more led by the adults than we had wanted, but the learning that took place afterwards made the unexpected intervention worthwhile.

Back in the classroom the children made spiders, drew and painted webs, looked at the patterns on spiders and examined pictures of the different types of webs.

3 November

Introducing children to forest school

All early years settings and school reception classes will have well-planned, tried and tested transition processes, and how you introduce children to your forest school environment needs to be dealt with in the same meticulous way. Taking account of many factors and showing patience and flexibility are the keys to a successful integration.

The first and foremost consideration will be the children. How old are they? What prior experiences have they had? Do any of your group have specific needs that will impact on the level of provision?

Where is your provision? Are you based in a rural or urban area? This will affect the experiences your children have had in the past. For many young children growing up in towns and cities the idea of space and freedom away from specially designed playgrounds and parks will be new. They may not have experienced opportunities to wear wellington boots, play in the rain or dig in the mud. For children from more rural localities you may well be surprised how many of them don't have the freedom you might expect. Many rural families are isolated and all movement between the home and the outside world may be done in the car, limiting the children's experiences of the changing weather and seasons.

When you have an agreed forest school zone you will need to ensure you have met the health and safety requirements and that your staff are competent and enthusiastic. Are they as well prepared as the children, with the correct clothing and footwear?

With a dedicated space, correct staffing and your forest school kit bag you can begin your visits. Consider how the children can be introduced gradually. Although forest school is known for its outdoors in all weathers approach, maybe the coldest, wettest day of the autumn is not the right start! Make the first visit fun and exciting, playing '1, 2, 3, where are you?' is a great way to explore the space safely and with an adult close by.

Make your initial visits short, keep the groups smaller and the activities simple and free-flow. Ensure the children know the basic rules and reinforce them gently throughout each visit. Set a routine that you can follow on each visit. It may start in the setting; toilet visit, boots and coats on, rule reminders and an appropriate song. These routines will become familiar for the children and will offer security for the majority of children.

Keep the parents informed about your visits, perhaps after the first session you could hold an open afternoon where the children can show pictures and share their excitement?

TO DO

- Forest school will have been up and running for a few weeks by now so check your kit bag and first-aid kit. Replenish and replace wherever necessary.
- Continue to add boxes to your resource area. Ask the children to what they would like to have access. Can any of the resources complement the themes in your setting?
- Consider how you will be making assessments whilst you are outdoors. Think about variety: written notes, photos, children's comments, film footage etc. Share these ideas and plans with all staff involved and share the assessment workload.

November at forest school

Children in most settings will have settled into their new routines by now, reception classes will be full-time and nursery children will be enjoying their new sessions with more confidence. If you have been using forest school since early autumn your children will be enjoying more freedom and will already have a bank of ideas for their time outside.

Make sure that the parents continue to support their children with the correct clothing and footwear. Remind them to check foot sizes; children grow out of boots very quickly!

The planning in this chapter is more about the season of autumn and preparation for winter. The children will have the chance to explore their surroundings through the eyes of the wildlife they share it with.

The correct clothing and footwear is essential for all forest school participants.

Sending home information about these activities will continue to involve the parents in your day-to-day tasks. Perhaps they can carry out some of the same activities at home, begin feeding the birds through the winter or make a simple hedgehog home.

If you have any favourite websites that you use for inspiration consider sharing them with your parents.

All about hedgehogs

> **Objectives**
>
> - To begin to know and name some of the wildlife with which we share the outdoor area.
> - To be able to talk about, and are excited about, the changes in the season.
> - To know what the word hibernate means.

Adult initiated ideas

Introduce the children to the word, hibernate. Perhaps some of them have heard it before. What animals do we know that hibernate? Which of these may live in our forest school? There are only three British mammals that truly hibernate – bats, dormice and hedgehogs – but frogs, toads and newts also disappear for the winter. The children may have experiences of non-native animals that sleep through winter, tortoises and bears being the most frequently known about.

Ask the children to make somewhere for your native hedgehogs to stay warm through the winter. Leaf and stick piles in sheltered places would make good homes. Gathering the fallen leaves and piling them up will keep the children happy for the whole session!

Harry thought the hedgehogs would need lots of leaves to stay warm.

Harry's hedgehog home.

Thinking about wild food

> **Objectives**
>
> - To know that some animals hide their food for the winter months.
> - To know the kinds of food that these animals might be looking for.
> - To provide feeding stations for these creatures.

Adult initiated ideas

Remind the children that some animals go to sleep for the winter and therefore don't need much food once they are asleep. Talk about animals and birds that may find it hard to find food. Do the children know why it is hard for them to find food?

Have you got any squirrels living in your area? Have the children seen them in nearby parks and wild areas?

Discuss what squirrels eat and talk about how they make sure they have enough food for the winter. Explain that they are vegetarian, eating foods such as nuts, apples, bark, seeds, fruits, buds, pine cones, mushrooms, roots, leaves and twigs. Most of these foods are in great supply in the autumn. Talk about how the squirrels bury food so they can find it again.

Set up a simple feeding station that contains some of these foods, including corn on the cob. Ask the children to draw the animals they think will visit their food supplies. If possible create a small hide for the children to sit in. They might not see the squirrels collecting food but they will be surprised to see the birds that come along.

Feeding the wild birds

Objectives

- To consider the types of food that visiting birds will like to eat.
- To choose food stuff to use in their bird feeders.
- To learn to watch quietly in order to see wildlife in action.

Adult initiated ideas

Remind the children about why squirrels stash food and relate it to birds also needing enough energy through the winter. Explain that we can help the birds by supplying them with regular food.

Share pictures of the birds you might expect to see. Can the children name any of them?

Set up several opportunities for children to make some simple bird feeders.

1 Mix lard or dripping with breadcrumbs, grated cheese and bird seed. Thread some string through a small yoghurt pot and fill it with the mixture. Alternatively tie some string to a pine cone and spread the mixture around the cone.
2 Cut a length of wire and bend one end. Thread hooped cereal, bread chunks and fruit onto the wire and make a hook at the other end. These wire feeders can be wound into hoops or linked together to make a chain of food.
3 Clean out some cardboard milk cartons and cut up a window in one side about 2cm from the bottom. Thread a hanging loop through the top and put your chosen bird food in the bottom.

Encourage the children to make observations about the visitors they see.

Ethan mixed seeds with lard to make his bird food.

Then he put it into a bird feeder.   Ethan's feeder was hung with others.

Observing the birds

Objectives

- To use their forest school practical and observation skills to learn more about their outdoor area.
- To know how to make a space that will help them stay hidden from the birds.
- To work as part of a group to create a finished bird hide.

Adult initiated ideas

Supply the children with large camouflage sheets and netting, string, rope and jumbo pegs. Help them create a small den, from which they can see their feeding stations.

Place pictures and labels of birds inside, a camera, clipboards, binoculars, paper and pencils. Encourage the children to record what they see. Talk about how the children will need to behave in order for anything to visit the food; can the children stay still and quiet enough?

As you try out this activity more often you may add to the materials you use in the bird hide: photos of previous visitors, home-made binoculars and warm/waterproof floor covering.

You may need to take smaller groups to the area for this activity. If possible, the rest of the group could be working in a different area — quietly!

Ruby wondered if the birds would eat the leftover cakes.

Oscar saw some birds in the hedge beyond the fence which he asked to feed as well.

Child initiated ideas

After you have introduced the feeding station, provide the resources for the children to initiate this themselves. Include books and posters about the animals and birds they are feeding.

Keep the den building resources nearby so that the children can make themselves, dens, hibernation homes etc.

Leaf collecting tools: brooms, a selection of different sized buckets, leaf scoops, wheelbarrows and large bags.

A box of cut-off timber, decking pieces, logs and wooden bricks.

Wax crayons and charcoal, paper and card, pressed leaves and bark pieces.

The children threaded food onto garden wire and made some more feeders that could hang outside the classroom.

RESOURCES

Adult initiated ideas:

- Forest school kit bag
- Forest school first-aid kit
- Books: fiction and non-fiction, about hibernating hedgehogs, bats and dormice
- Pictures of these animals
- Pictures and books about squirrels in winter
- If you can find any, it is interesting for the children to look at pine cones and nuts that have been eaten by the squirrels
- A large tree stump to make your feeding station

- Selection of food for wildlife, nuts, seeds, fruit, corn on the cob etc.
- Bird feeders: homemade or bought
- Garden wire, string etc.
- Bird food (seeds, fruit, cereal, raisins, lard or dripping, bread, grated cheese etc.)
- Small yoghurt pots, pine cones etc.
- Small milk cartons
- Camouflage net and den covers
- Large pegs, rope and string
- Binoculars, garden and wild bird pictures and books
- Blankets and waterproof cover for the floor
- Paper and pencils
- Camera

Case study

Traditionally we have a cohort of children who are very familiar with their local environment, and whilst there are usually one or two children who have less experience of the outdoors the majority are very at home in our forest area.

Introducing the idea that animals might sleep through the winter was interesting. Very few children knew which ones they might be. We did, however, have one child who knew a lot about hibernating dormice. It transpired that his Mum worked for the local wildlife trust monitoring the dormouse population in a small piece of local woodland.

Following our sessions about hibernation she came into school with a large collection of resources for the children to explore; a dormouse nest, nuts with teeth marks on, pictures, hibernation boxes and a real dormouse. We were able to explain to the children that the young dormouse had been rescued and was living in an outbuilding, with a regular supply of food to help him fatten up. Mum explained he was unlikely to hibernate that year.

The little boy was very proud that he and his Mum knew more about dormice than we did and his self-esteem clearly improved over these few sessions. His Mum, having enjoyed her visit, volunteered to help weekly and became a very valued member of our team, sharing her wealth of knowledge with us all.

Monthly blog

We had always encouraged the children in our groups to look out for and identify the creatures, birds and animals around them, so feeding the birds was not a new activity. We have bird tables and feeders in the playground, so some of the children are already learning about bird names and habits.

Taking the bird feeding activity to our forest area was new to us and did create some logistical difficulties with transporting all the resources, but the children were happy to help carry our emergency food parcel.

Once in the outdoor area, with numerous bird feeders in situ we all helped to create the bird hide. The children were enthusiastic about what they wanted inside, and a few journeys were made to gather more blankets and cushions.

The biggest problem we encountered was the amount of noise the rest of the children were making at the other end of the area. However quiet the children in the hide were, the noise from the others meant that no birds came to the area. After a day or two we noticed the food was being eaten, so we decided to visit the area with just a small group wanting to watch the birds. This was far more successful and soon we were having regular recorded visitors. This kept the children much more motivated and there was a surge of interest in the food being put on the bird table outside the classroom. A display of pictures and posters enabled us to share our sightings with the rest of the school and the parents.

4 December

Forest school routines

Every setting will need to adopt their own appropriate routines, but here I have outlined the procedures that we have found work for us. When you are establishing your own routines it is important that you take into account the unique factors affecting your site. This should include the location of the outdoor area, your means of arriving at it, the age of the children, your group size and the adults you have with you. You will already have made risk assessments and have policies for health and safety of the children and the activities you are carrying out. You may need to take account of the weather, although routines should be regular and frequent and not change too much, so consider whether you can overcome the weather-related issues without disruption.

Our routine starts in the morning, in the classroom, when all children check they have brought their kit to school. We keep wellies at school and encourage parents to keep outdoor kit bags there to, but checking in the morning gives us a chance to chase any missing kits. This also reminds the children that we are going to forest school, and usually sets a buzz about what they want to do.

Then, when appropriate, the children get changed and outdoor coats and waterproofs are gathered in one place. Following toilet visits the children put on their outer layers and their wellies and wait outside on the benches until everyone is ready.

Some of the kit will already be in the forest area, the rest of it is shared between children and adults and taken with us; this includes the drinks and snacks. As we leave the premises we will inform the office staff where we will be and confirm we have phones with us.

We reach our area by crossing a large playing field, halfway we stop and stand in a circle. The children are encouraged to recall the forest school rules and they are reinforced with the reasoning behind them. Then they are free to run to the gateway. One of our rules is that they don't enter without an adult, so they wait for us to catch up. Once inside we always start in the log circle, here we explain the activities and the resources available today and the children are sent off to take up whatever they want.

When they are needed back, an adult calls 'log circle' and they return. They quickly remember they have drinks and snacks as we are finishing the session and during this time we have a discussion about what they have been doing. We have found that having drinks too early in the session results in several toilet visits!

As we leave we share out the resources again and return across the field. We have a stopping point so that the children don't arrive at the car park unaccompanied.

Back outside the classroom, the children quickly learn the order of going back; wellies off and carried back to the rack, coats off and sit in a circle on the carpet.

Having such a set routine helps all the children settle quickly. There are few surprises each week apart from new experiences once we arrive and the less confident children are happier when they are clear about what is happening and when.

As mentioned, make your routine personal and consistent, so that even if a different person is leading the group, the session is similar enough to maintain happy and well-behaved children.

TO DO

- Continue to make and record observations of all your children. Check that you are covering a range of learning areas over several different occasions. Identify any patterns of learning, schemas, specific learning interests and styles and adapt your planning to make allowances for these forest school sessions.

- Bring the outdoors inside if the weather turns particularly wintry. But don't stop your outdoor visits; shorten them and make them active and fun so that everyone stays warm.

- If your setting celebrates Christmas look at how you can use the natural resources to make decorations and presents.

- Draw an outline of the planning for next term. Take into account the potential weather, the number and confidence of your children, the ability of the staff and volunteers. Share your ideas and encourage others to add their suggestions. Make sure any key workers have included anything they feel necessary and specific to their children.

December at forest school

The outdoor environment can look very sparse in the month of December; the autumn leaves have begun to decompose and the trees are completely bare. The undergrowth will have died down and you will rediscover big areas of land that perhaps have been inaccessible. The children will enjoy the chance to traipse through what is usually the nettle patch, or hide deeper into the hedges without worrying about stinging themselves.

Our outdoor classroom can be very bland and bare during the winter months, but it provides a changing environment in which to explore.

Sparse undergrowth provides new opportunities for exploration.

If you are a regular fire lighter then consider where you can dry and store some logs and kindling before it gets beyond use. The children enjoy bundling kindling and stacking small logs so incorporate this into the regular activities on offer.

Sonnie had chosen his firewood but wanted to make it the same size as his arm, to comply with our rule.

He was joined by another member of the class who showed him how to break the stick down.

Having broken his stick, Sonnie checked it was no longer than the length of his arm.

In many UK settings children will be celebrating Christmas. You will find a vast array of decorations and ideas for outdoor play that will support this occasion, by using the Internet. The planning for this month includes ideas for some elements of Christmas, but does not go into great detail. Instead, it focuses on using the fallen sticks and readily available natural materials. Some items may have to be gathered from elsewhere and brought to your site. We don't have the advantage of any evergreen trees, so I regularly collect bundles of pine branches and cones for use at forest school. You may find that your parents are happy to help with this process, but be sure to think ahead so that the materials are there when you need them.

Mud painting

Objectives

- To identify the changes to the trees and plants during the winter.
- To use mud, paint and natural materials to make pictures.
- To explore texture and shape.

Adult initiated ideas

Ask the children to look at the trees and plants. What has happened? Talk about the bare trees, the shapes of them and the colour of the bark and branches.

Supply some paint and help the children turn mud into paint by adding water. Ask the children to paint pictures of the trees, thinking about the overall shape of the trees and the way the branches are linked.

To challenge the children don't supply brushes, let them find their own tools. They will probably use sticks, but you could introduce some evergreen branches, stones, pine cones etc.

Hang the pictures on the washing line, or fix them to the trees to dry out. Encourage the children to use the camera to photograph their tree as well. Back in the setting the pictures can be printed and added to the paintings.

This child found a paintbrush that had been left behind and used it to paint mud on the trees.

The children mixed their own mud paint. This is a picture of our outdoor classroom.

This little boy used his 'paint' to draw a picture of his Daddy.

Making a storytelling stick

> **Objectives**
> - To retell a familiar story.
> - To use the environment and its resources to support retelling the story.
> - To persevere in an activity to produce their own end result.

Adult initiated ideas

Before this session the children will need to be familiar with a simple tale. It could be a story that is well known or one you have been working on inside. It is more successful if the story has repeated phrases that the children already know. For example: 'I'll huff and I'll puff and blow your house down', from the story of The Three Little Pigs.

Share a story stick you have already made and demonstrate how the children can make their own.

A story stick helps the owner remember and retell events or stories to others. The idea is that items are gathered and added to the stick to use as reminders for key parts of the story.

Supply rope, string, sticky-tape and pipe cleaners for fixing materials.

Working in a small group these girls went to find items to help retell the story of The Three Bears.

This story stick tells the story of The Three Little Pigs. The fir cones represented the houses and the flower was picked in one of the gardens!

Making natural mobiles

> **Objectives**
>
> - To use natural materials to make hanging decorations.
> - To practise the skills required for tying and fixing.
> - To work with a partner or adult, sharing ideas and skills.

Adult initiated ideas

Talk about the kinds of decorations the children may have been hanging at home or in your setting in preparation for Christmas and suggest the children may like to make their own to decorate one of the outdoor area trees.

Have a selection of pre made examples available to promote ideas.

Provide a large selection of additional natural materials and remind the children about the resources already around them.

Help the children tie some sticks into a simple triangle and add the items they wish. The age of the children you are working with, and their prior experience, will determine how independent they can be in this process. I have found that children can usually twist and fix using pipe cleaners if they find tying tricky. Alternatively they can wrap the string around the items and a nearby adult can assist with the fixing.

Choose a tree with low branches and encourage the children to fix their decoration by themselves. An adult can surreptitiously fix the items more securely if necessary.

Tying sticks together is challenging for young children. This child was focused on his task for some time and was very proud when he managed to tie several sticks together to make his mobile.

We hang completed mobiles and stick bundles on our 'washing line'.

Winter decorations

> ### Objectives
>
> - To make a traditional decoration using evergreen materials.
> - To begin to understand that people have different beliefs and traditions.
> - To recognise that many of our own beliefs started a long time ago.

Adult initiated ideas

Talk to the children about the historic aspects of house decorating at Christmas. Discuss how the children decorate their own homes and what they use. Many children may have got their own, or seen, Christmas trees. Talk about how these trees have needles that stay all winter. Show some other materials that stay green all year.

If you have been working on some traditional tales talk about the bad characters and explain that people used to hang evergreen branches to keep them away.

Provide a large quantity of evergreen materials and some string and ask the children to make their own decoration to take home with them.

A really effective decoration can be made with a few evergreen branches.

Child initiated ideas

- Provide the den building kit, add extra blankets and cushions for warmth and comfort.
- A basket of fixing materials, string, rope, pipe cleaners etc.
- A log basket for wood collecting.
- Painting materials, large sheets or rolls of paper fixed to a fence.

RESOURCES

Adult initiated ideas:

- Forest school kit bag
- Forest school first-aid kit
- Paint, pots, spoons and stirrers
- Evergreen branches, pine cones, stones and sticks
- Paper
- Camera
- Pegs for hanging
- Long sticks, about 1 metre, 1 per child
- Fixing kit, string, rope, sticky-tape, pipe cleaners, garden wire, scissors
- Imported natural materials
- Examples of pre-made hanging decorations

Case study

We often have elements of painting in our outdoor play, but traditionally we have always offered brushes. The process of removing the brushes began when, on one afternoon when one little boy in our group discovered an abandoned paint brush and started painting the nearby tree with the mud from a puddle. Other children wanted to join him, but there were no more brushes so they decided to use sticks instead. They spent some time scooping the mud up on the end of their sticks and wiping it onto the tree. On the following visit the children returned to the paint sticks without prompting.

One child, Ellie, was particularly interested in how much mud she could balance on her stick and when reaching the tree spread it over the whole area she could reach. When the rest of the tree became out of reach, she dropped her stick and returned some time later with a longer one. She continued painting until the reachable area was covered too. This went on several times and on each return the stick was a little longer.

Then on one visit back she returned with a stick that was almost as tall as her. One of the other children in the group told her the stick was too long and she shouldn't have it (the rule is the stick should be no longer than your arm unless you have help).

Together the two children broke the stick and took a piece each. Ellie started to paint the tree again, but it was clear she couldn't reach the area she had been trying to get to. At this stage she came to me and asked if I could do it for her. I agreed I could paint the top, if she would finish the lower parts. She was happy with this arrangement and over the next few minutes we successfully layered mud across the bark.

Ellie has been very sensible about the stick rule and clearly understood the boundaries. By approaching a nearby adult she was able to complete the task she had set out to do without breaking the rules.

Using a stick to make pictures in the outdoor classroom.

Monthly blog

The observational tree painting that we did this month threw up some interesting ideas. The children were very aware that the leaves had all fallen and knew from previous visits that the trees would grow leaves again. We had a long conversation about the branches, with the children noticing that they each came from a different branch, rather than all from the trunk.

Feeling positive about their observation skills they set about painting using their own choice of paint and implements. Initially the trees were quite successfully painted and looked remarkably like the winter trees we could see.

Then one of the children returned to the area with green paint he had taken from the shed. He proceeded to cover his winter tree in green leaves! Some of the other children, noticing what he was doing, did the same. It is one of those difficult situations where we weren't sure whether we should intervene. It was clear these children wanted leafy trees, but the objective was that they paint the winter ones.

We allowed them to paint their trees green and then talked in a small group about their pictures. Some of the children had done it because 'he did'! One of them told me they had got the tree 'dressed' because it looked cold and the first little boy had done it because trees have leaves.

Some of the children chose to add green leaves to their trees.

The children were all praised for their hard work and finished paintings and asked if they would like another turn. They all agreed and the green paint was quickly removed. On the second occasion the children painted the winter trees that they could see.

When they were all hung on the fence, the paintings actually created a talking point among the group, with discussion about summer leaves and the bare branches. There was further talk about how the trees looked different again when their trees were brown in the autumn.

More paintings were added to the selection and an interesting display of trees through the seasons appeared.

5 January

The adult role at forest school

On each visit to forest school it is the adults who can make or break the session. It is their enthusiasm that rubs off on the children and when the weather is cold and damp this positive attitude is absolutely essential. If the children overhear the adults complaining about cold feet it stands to reason that they are likely to complain too! Adults accompanying the children need to be aware that they can inadvertently have a negative impact on the session.

Well-planned lessons, with each adult having a clear role, will help to keep everyone busy, therefore ensuring less opportunity for negativity to spread.

Adults should be well-trained in the purpose of learning outdoors; they will quickly learn to notice when and where learning is taking place and should know how to record any significant experiences they witness. They must understand and adhere to the health and safety rules at all times, enforcing them clearly with the children. Qualified and experienced members of staff will recognise the importance of using praise with children and should use this to build self-esteem and confidence in the children with whom they are working. Allowing children a degree of independence is also crucial. In many forest school activities the children should be able to lead their own play, but in the early stages they will need more encouragement to become more sure about their ability.

To sum up, the adults need to be positive at all times, able to encourage independence and skilled at recognising learning and developing it further.

TO DO

- Check the condition of the outdoor area. Does any of it need fencing off to prevent long-term damage to the environment?
- Remind parents to ensure the clothing they are supplying is warm and weatherproof.
- Have a surplus of ideas to ensure the weather conditions can add to the experiences offered.
- Identify gaps in observations and assessments and plan experiences to fill them.
- Check and update risk assessment, in particular fire safety.
- Inform parents of the anticipated learning and offer ideas that will help them support the children at home.

January at forest school

January is a challenging time of year in the outdoor environment. Both adults and children are more susceptible to the cold and damp conditions and it is likely that well-organised and thought-out sessions will need to be adapted to take into account the weather conditions.

This month the planning looks at developing the children's understanding, skills and awareness of fires and fire lighting. At this point in the year the new children have already been visiting forest school for a significant amount of time and for most the everyday rules and expectations are well-embedded. Adding new guidelines about fire safety is crucial and ensuring all children have understood them needs to be monitored closely by all staff.

This series of lessons requires the outdoor area to have a safe fire-lighting area. The usual forest school approach to this is to make a small fire area in the centre of some cleared ground. The fire area itself should be contained within four large logs, preferably not too dead – this should prevent them burning too readily.

The outer edge of this cleared area needs some fixed logs to create both a sitting area and a boundary. The children will be taught not to walk inside this log circle, which should be approximately two to three metres away from the fire.

A quick check of the area on each visit should be made with specific focus on the safety of this area, including any overhanging branches too close to the fire.

In order to light several fires over the series of lessons, you will need to ensure that there is an ample supply of sticks for the children to collect. In some instances these may be brought to the area and distributed for the children to collect when necessary. You will also need to gather green wood if it is not easily available for the children to independently collect it.

Having made this visual risk assessment you will need to consider whether any additional rules need to be in place for that session.

Children are taught very early on to stay a safe distance from the fire area at all times.

Fire safety

> **Objectives**
>
> - To introduce the children to the experience of lighting fires safely.
> - To provide opportunities for children to discuss their own experiences of fire.
> - To talk about the need for rules that keep all of us safe around fires.

Adult initiated ideas

Lead a discussion about fire safety. This should include all the rules the children need to remember. These could also be provided in the form of a laminated key fob, using symbols to remind the children. Different sites will need their own 'site specific' rules.

Show the children how we use matches to light a fire and water or sand to put it out again. If you feel it appropriate, introduce the Fire Triangle. We need fuel (wood), heat (matches) and oxygen (air) to build a fire.

Do the children know what would happen if one of these elements was removed?

Collecting firewood

> **Objectives**
>
> - To collect fuel to light a fire.
> - To understand that all wood is not the same.
> - To know that wet wood does not burn because it contains some moisture/water.

Adult initiated ideas

Show the children some sticks of varying lengths and from different trees. Some should be dead wood collected from the ground and others should be cut from living trees. Ask the children to examine the sticks and use lots of words to describe them to each other. Settle on an appropriate word that describes both dead and live wood. Forest school favourites are 'snappy' and 'bendy'.

Why do the children think that the live wood is bendy? Explain that living plants contain water to keep them alive. Does this mean the bendy wood will burn well or not? Put some of each on the fire and watch them burn. This can lead to discussion about smoke, crackling, which burns the quickest etc.

Send the children to find wood that is snappy and bring it back for the fire. It may be useful to give the children a size limit, for example, as thick as your finger, as long as your arm.

Collecting firewood is an important job on every visit.

Children learn to bundle the sticks, ready to be hung up to dry.

Charcoal making

Objectives

- To know that fire can be used to change the properties of materials.
- To make predictions about the changes they may see.
- To make observations about the changes they observe.

Adult initiated ideas

Sitting in the log circle remind the children about the fire safety rules and explain that we can use the fire to change various items.

Do the children know what charcoal is? Discuss. Some of them may be aware that it is used on barbecues. Explain that it is burnt wood and show some examples. Why do the children think there are holes in the tin? What will happen to the sticks we put inside?

Our charcoal tin is an old biscuit tin. Before using it with the children it needs a little preparation. Punch several holes in the lid so that the steam can escape without blowing the lid off. You should then burn the tin over a fire until all the paint is burnt off. It will smell quite strongly, but not for long. When you use the tin it is crucial that you are health and safety aware. The tin will be very hot after it is removed from the fire, you will also find it hard to remove the lid until it has had a chance to cool off. As long as you are careful and explain your actions there is very little that can go wrong. It is clearly an activity that needs to be adult led, although when the charcoal has cooled the children will enjoy examining the changes that have taken place.

The charcoal tin needs to be placed in the heat of the fire.

The children are always fascinated by the metallic colours of the finished charcoal.

Willow, hazel or elder make good charcoal sticks. Cut the small twigs from a tree and place inside the charcoal tin, safely placing the tin on the fire using fireproof gloves. While the children are watching they should see smoke coming from the holes in the tin lid. The charcoal can take anything from ten minutes to thirty depending on the strength of the fire.

When it is black, take the tin off the fire and allow it to cool down. Pass some charcoal sticks to the children and encourage them to paint their own faces and the backs of their hands.

Children love putting on charcoal war paint!

Cooking over a fire

> **Objectives**
>
> - To know that fire creates heat that can be used to change the properties of some foods.
> - To know how to approach the fire safely.
> - To cook their own snack over the fire.

Adult initiated ideas

Remind the children about the fire safety rules. While the fire is being lit ask the children to collect some firewood to keep it going. Give them a size limit, for example, no longer than their arm, as thick as their finger.

When all the children have gathered back at the lit fire, introduce a rule about approaching the fire: only approach when invited and accompanied by an adult; return to their log quickly and safely following cooking; do not go back to the fire.

Easy foods to start with when cooking on a fire include, bread, crumpets, tea cakes, marshmallows etc. These foods can be pushed onto a stick and held over the hot embers. The longer the cooking stick the further away the children can stay. The children should approach with an adult and be shown how to kneel close to the fire.

Depending on the size of the group, this can take quite a long time. You have several choices: all the children can stay and watch or half the group can go away to explore. The children left at the fire could lead some singing.

> We've all been to forest school, forest school, forest school;
> we've all been to forest school on this cold and windy/hot and sunny day.
> (Sung to the tune 'Here we go round the mulberry bush.')

Variations could be: 'We've been drinking hot chocolate', 'We can cook around the fire', 'We have collected lots of sticks' etc. 'She'll be coming through the forest when she comes' etc., sung to the tune 'She'll be coming round the mountain when she comes.'

Once again the children will enjoy adding their own words. For example: 'She'll be cooking toasted tea cakes when she comes', 'She'll be sitting in the circle when she comes', 'She'll be warming by the fire when she comes'.

Child initiated ideas

These sessions clearly detail the kinds of activities you can do with the children around the theme of fire lighting, but they are all adult initiated. This next section suggests some child-led activities that can be set up or prepared in order to encourage the children to play and explore independently during their visit to the outdoor classroom.

- Make a mock fire, collecting and piling sticks in a fire shape.
- Make hedgehog dens using fallen sticks.
- Tie sticks together to make a hanging decoration/mobile.
- Make pictures on the floor using sticks.
- Sort sticks according to size, length, colour etc.

The fire doesn't need to be large to cook over, but it will need to well alight before you start.

Cooking marshmallows is a favourite treat in our outdoor classroom.

Soup can be cooking over the fire while children busy themselves with other activities.

RESOURCES

Adult initiated ideas:

- Forest school first-aid kit
- Forest school drinks
- Laminated set of fire safety rules
- Fire lighting kit (matches/lighter, firelighter, newspaper, dry kindling)
- Fire water or sand bucket
- Examples of charcoal – chunks and sticks
- Small hazel, willow or elder twigs
- Charcoal tin
- Fireproof gloves
- Food for cooking (teacakes, bread, crumpets, marshmallows etc.)

Child initiated ideas:

- String and rope of varying lengths and thickness
- Scissors
- A selection of objects and natural materials for exploration
- A box of fabric and waterproof cloth
- Trowels and buckets

Case study

The children had already been given an introduction to the fire and the log circle and were clear about the safety rules surrounding that area of the outdoor classroom. On this occasion, the third session, the children were sitting in the log circle discussing the fire. They had noticed that the fire was many different colours and were calling them out as they saw them.

The assistant watching the fire poked some of the logs around which unearthed some of the larger logs covered in white ash. This led to a conversation about which was the hottest part of the fire. The vast majority of the children believed it to be the flames. Most of the others thought it would be the sticks that were glowing, but one child was adamant that it was the white sticks at the bottom. He was unable to explain why, but this did lead to a discussion about how we could find out.

Children are fascinated by the fire and are often quite happy to sit and watch the flames.

The responses included: touching the fire in different places, which led to more discussion about safety; putting more sticks on to see where they burnt the quickest; and eventually someone suggested we should see what happened if we put something on each area.

After some general discussion about what we could put onto the fire the children agreed that cooking something would be a good idea.

This prompted a planning session for our outdoor classroom time the next week.

Monthly blog

This series of lessons was successfully delivered; although due to some unexpected snowfall, two of the sessions were pushed together in order to reach the cooking finale.

Snow in our part of the UK is relatively unusual and it could not be ignored just because it wasn't planned for. The children loved the snow, using buckets and spades to relocate it all over the school field. We will be able to use these experiences to support some planned opportunities in February.

The children enjoyed a rare and unexpected fall of snow.

The children showed great maturity around the fire area, although on each visit there was one child who needed closer adult supervision to ensure he didn't wander into the log circle. I quickly allocated a member of staff to stay close to him during the session.

The cooking was the highlight of the lessons, although it always presents us with many children waiting for their turn. We overcame this by sending children away to gather more sticks and tie them into bundles. They enjoyed tying these bundles up to dry ready for a future visit. We use a piece of rope strung between two trees as our 'washing line' onto which we can tie our stick bundles. By splitting the group into smaller groups to reduce the waiting time, we also spread our adults a little thin, but by keeping everyone within sight of the fire area, all children were supervised.

Incorporating cooking into future units is necessary to reinforce much of the learning that has taken place this month.

Risk at forest school

One of the underlying principles of any forest school is to introduce an element of risk into children's play experiences. This risk is always carefully monitored and thoroughly assessed by the adults leading the session. But from the children's perspective it is their decision-making and activities that determine their own level of achievement.

Children live in a world where many seemingly dangerous and risky activities are curtailed by the supervising adults or the organisation involved. Tight health and safety requirements have removed many of the opportunities that provide potential for children to fail and learn from their mistakes. In their everyday lives children are cosseted with safety matting, low-level play equipment or soft bats and balls. Whilst we all want our children to stay safe and well, it is vital that they grow up recognising their own limitations and learning to keep themselves safe. For that to happen they need to make mistakes and learn how to modify their own behaviour to prevent harm to themselves and their playmates.

A forest school reintroduces some of the danger into children's daily play. These risks are calculated and must be deemed acceptable for the age range of the children working in that session. For younger children an acceptable risk may be to allow them to explore without an adult in sight, or to climb the lower branches of a tree. Older children may be taught to use tools safely and independently, or to play on a well secured rope swing without support.

The level of risk is always determined by the ability of the children and the confidence of the forest school team. The important element of allowing risk is that it is assessed by the adults, but that the children believe it to be chancy and exciting.

Risk assessment should be carried out by the leader of the session and may take the form of either annual, daily, weekly or spontaneous decisions. Generally the area used for forest school should be well assessed, taking into account the age and number of children, the adult:child ratio, the types of regular activities and the available resources. This may include the area boundaries, the fire pit, open water etc. Activities are likely to include the use of tools, rope and sticks or branches. Spontaneous risk assessment may be required during the child's own free play, such as the collection of bugs, the use of mud or because of the weather conditions.

It stands to reason therefore that risk assessment may take the form of either written forms or oral decisions. In the case of oral or spontaneous assessment, it would be good practice to follow up the decision by completing a risk assessment form on return to the setting. This would help in the future when having to make similar decisions.

TO DO

- Provide parents with details of upcoming sessions, including the need for additional clothing.
- Make a photo book that documents the activities and which can be used back in the setting.
- Clear out old resources and tidy everyday activity boxes.

February at forest school

This set of planning takes advantage of the wintry weather conditions, allowing the children a chance to get outside and explore the cold conditions that often prevail in February. It gives suggestions for ice and snow play, encouraging the children to look more closely at the changing environment. It is vital to remember that very young children get cold quickly and with this in mind the session time might need shortening. It is also useful to have extra warm clothes for the children who are perhaps less prepared, to enable them to have a positive experience as well.

But with the unpredictable weather in the UK there are also ideas for using tools and making simple things from natural resources. However, these activities are often quite static, so opportunities for child-initiated play should be ample and varied, so the children are fully occupied while they wait for their turn.

The most important element of this month is to take account of the changing and widely diverse weather you are likely to encounter. Consider additional hazards such as snow, ice and frozen water. These should not be seen as obstacles, rather as new experiences. Young children learning to walk on icy ground find out about balance and caution, they are also likely to learn that frozen ground hurts when you land on it!

If you have a pond area that becomes frozen, rather than stay away from it, use it as an opportunity to discuss the hazards of frozen water and introduce some rules to keep the children safe.

Talk about how birds and animals keep warm during these cold periods and explore how feeding the birds or providing a shelter for a hibernating hedgehog can help them survive until the spring.

Consider how you will keep the children warm on the coldest days:

- Take a flask of hot drink.
- Take spare clothes, socks, gloves, hats and scarves.
- Could the children wear old training shoes, rather than wellies?
- Perhaps some wheat bags could be heated before the visit and kept for the coldest hands and feet.
- Shorten the sessions to help keep the experience positive.

Ice and snow

> **Objectives**
>
> - To take advantage of the winter weather to explore snow and ice in a variety of ways.
> - To begin to explore how snow and ice melts.
> - To encourage children to examine frost, snow and ice, looking for patterns.

Adult initiated ideas

Lead a conversation about the weather. What can the children tell you about it? Encourage them to share their own experiences of the cold, either in the setting or elsewhere. Ask open questions to promote the use of appropriate vocabulary: cold, freezing, icy, white, fluffy etc.

Provide ample opportunity for the children to explore and play freely, ensuring they are well prepared for the cold. Draw attention to the footprints they might be leaving in the snow. Has anything else left footprints? Draw pictures and take photos of the prints to use back at the setting.

Provide a resource box with magnifying glasses and a camera for the children to use independently. Does the frost make different patterns on the grass than it does on the fence?

Making ice hangers

> **Objectives**
>
> - To consider how water freezes.
> - To explore how ice melts.
> - To make frozen objects for examining.

Adult initiated ideas

Do the children know what has happened to the water? Talk about and share ideas about why the water has gone hard. Introduce the correct language, appropriate for the age group.

Allow the children plenty of time to explore the ice. How can they break it/melt it? Will it always be ice? Why not and what will help it melt? What happens when they hold the ice?

Light a small fire and promote discussion about warming the ice to melt it. Place some ice around the outside of the fire and encourage the children to observe from a safe distance.

Send the children to look for more ice and return to place it in a pan. Talk about what will happen if the pan is put over the fire. Do they know what will be left in the pan when it has got warm?

Back in the setting, fill some shallow containers with water and natural objects (if you add a length of string to each container the frozen objects can be hung up). Ask the –

children how we can turn them into ice. If it is cold enough, leave them out overnight, otherwise put them into a freezer for a couple of hours. When they are frozen hang them in different environments, asking the children for ideas and predictions about what will happen.

These children were keen to find out what would happen if they put their ice near the fire.

Making small hanging ice decorations gave the children an opportunity to see what happened to it during the day.

Using tools at forest school

These sessions provide alternative activities to allow for our unpredictable climate!

Objectives

- To introduce children to the uses of specific tools with very clear rules for safety.
- To allow the children to use tools under supervision, with regard to safety rules.

Adult initiated ideas

Introduce the children to your forest school tool bag and identify the various tools inside. Have the children seen any tools before? Where were they used and who was using them? Are they aware of any rules about using tools?

With the children's input, make some rules for the tool bag. They should include:

- Only use a tool with an adult's help.
- Do not help yourself to tools.
- Do not take tools away from the work area.
- Carry them in the way you have been shown.

Show the children how they are going to use a simple tool to make a utensil. Many forest school leaders now use potato peelers, rather than penknives for whittling. This is a personal choice and you should only introduce tools you are happy to use with the children. Whether you are using a peeler or a knife, they are both sharp and should be shown the same respect.

The children should always push the blade away from their body. If they push too hard they are likely to find the task quite difficult; a gentler touch usually works better. Work with the children on a ratio of one-to-one to make a stick (a metre long) with a pointed end. This can be used to cook something simple (marshmallow, banana, bread, crumpet etc.) at the end of the session.

Using tools takes a great deal of concentration.

More tools!

> ### Objectives
>
> - To introduce the children to a new tool, under adult guidance and strict safety rules.

Adult initiated ideas

Recap the tool safety rules created in the previous session and discuss the tools in the tool box. Show the children a saw; what is it used for? Do the children know the correct name for the teeth? Explain that it is the teeth that are sharp.

As with the previous session, work with the children on a one-to-one basis. Other children can be accessing child initiated play time, a safe distance from the tool area.

Guide the children through the process of sawing a log in half. Don't choose a log that has a very large diameter; make it achievable. Something about 3–5 cm is usually manageable. The children will enjoy looking at the end of their sawn log and exploring the rings and teeth marks. I always think it is a shame if the children don't take their log home, but I know others encourage the children to add it to the woodpile for the fire.

These children were happy to drag some more firewood to the outdoor classroom, but were quick to tell me it would take too long to saw it up.

There was a great deal of discussion about which logs would be suitable for sawing. In the end all of these were rejected for a smaller one.

Child initiated ideas

During the sessions where the children are exploring the weather-related changes to their environment there are several activities that the children will enjoy leading themselves. Of course, if the children are very confident they will be truly child initiated, but younger children in a new environment will benefit from some resources and ideas to get them started. Allow the children to use these props in the way that suits them and their style of learning.

- Set up a resource box filled with magnifiers of varying descriptions. You may be able to include some small handheld microscopes.
- Leave out some laminated pictures of frost and ice patterns, a camera, paper and pencils.
- Provide a selection of soft toys and dolls, with a basket of warm clothes to dress them in.
- Take some bottles and flasks of water, some warm and some cold.

RESOURCES

Adult initiated ideas:

- Forest school first-aid kit
- Forest school drinks
- Paper, pencils, crayons
- Magnifying glasses, handheld microscopes, camera and spare batteries
- Fire lighting kit and extinguishing water, saucepan
- Shallow containers – cake tins, ice cube trays, foil dishes etc.
- Natural materials, string, scissors
- Access to a freezer if necessary
- Tool bag, including penknives, potato peelers, appropriately sized saws and child sized gloves
- Sticks for whittling – 1 metre long, elder or hazel
- Branches for sawing – ½ metre long, 3–5cm diameter
- Food for cooking on sticks – marshmallows, banana, bread, crumpets etc.

Child initiated ideas:

- Resource box – magnifiers, microscopes, camera
- Laminated pictures of frost, ice, snow and snowflakes
- Box of soft toys and dolls and various items of outdoor clothing
- Bottles containing both warm and cold water
- Blankets and rugs
- Basket of hats and scarves
- Items for making imprints in the snow – large wooden or foam bricks, mega blocks, large 2d and 3d shapes

Case study

A group of children had discovered that a rather large puddle had frozen over since their last visit. They were standing around the outside when one child began to walk on the edge. The ice cracked under his feet and he jumped back again. A second child said he shouldn't stand on it because he would fall in and underneath it would be 'very tall and go all the way into the earth'. There followed a rather lively discussion about what was under the ice. None of the children were prepared to back down! Most of the group agreed it would be wet, one child thought it would be dry because all the water had 'gone into the ice'. The first child was still sure it would be so deep they would disappear.

Prompted by a nearby adult, the children began trying to break the ice by prodding it with sticks. This was futile and several of the children wandered off. The children that were left started kicking the ice around the edges where it eventually gave way. They were delighted to be able to pick pieces up and show each other. When they had removed enough they noticed that the ground underneath was hard mud. They began to jump on it in an attempt to break it. One child brought over a bottle of water to 'turn the puddle muddy again'. I was able to note his understanding of melting something frozen.

Monthly blog

The activities that introduce the children to the tool bag are an essential part of forest school practice and is well practised in this setting. The children were responsive to new rules, having successfully taken on the fire area rules over the previous few weeks.

It was apparent that the children were keen to use the tools, but unusually this group of children wanted to create an end result. I was glad I had considered using the sticks for cooking in the same session; this satisfied their design needs. They renamed their cooking sticks with a variety of interesting words – marshmallow holders, toasters, kebab sticks, spoons etc.!

Assessment at forest school

If forest school is to become part of your regular learning experiences in your setting it will need to be treated in the same way that other indoor opportunities are. Therefore, finding a way of assessing the children on their regular visits becomes essential. Often the unexpected happens and children show different and new behaviours in this diverse environment and it is important that these don't go unnoticed.

How much and what kind of assessment takes place needs to be decided upon among the practitioners taking part. There is no point in one person making decisions that affect everyone; this may, in fact, lead to ineffective assessment and poor follow-up routines. If the children are working at forest school with their key workers, these are the most informed people to make judgements about their own group of children.

Some settings prefer the forest school sessions to be documented religiously, others are happy to gather some appropriate photos and a few notes to add to a learning journey. It should be remembered that the revised EYFS suggests that paperwork should be reduced and must remain manageable. Writing up copious notes at the end of the session becomes a chore and will ultimately take away some of the enjoyment for the staff involved.

My suggestion is that staff take several cameras and take still and video shots throughout, which can be annotated and used to plan the child's next steps. It would also be sensible to limit the number of children you assess on each session, working from a rota that ensures all children are assessed over, perhaps a four-week period. Each week could have a different focus to narrow assessment down even further.

We gather evidence of learning over numerous visits, building a useful diary of the child's activities throughout the year.

TO DO

- Make and laminate some simple identification charts to help the children spot and name the new plants.
- Make some laminated labels with words and pictures, which the children can use to tag the new growth.
- Begin a photo book of spring changes recording the same trees and plants on each visit, building a picture of their growth over a period of weeks.
- Consider writing an online blog that will help the parents keep up with the coming of spring.
- Reassess the clothing the children have, ensuring it is suitable for the continually changing weather.

March at forest school

March is the month of new beginnings and whilst some spring flowers, such as snowdrops, are already in bloom many more plants and trees will now begin to change. Children should be encouraged to look for these differences on each of their visits. Sharing this information with parents as well might help the children to continue their observations in other environments. At this point in the academic year, children will have been visiting forest school regularly for several months and their confidence will have increased enormously. This will help the children to find their own play and learning experiences, allowing the adult to become more of a passive supporter rather than a full-time educator. But of course, children need to learn as well, so inspiring them to try new activities and use the correct language becomes more important. You are likely to have assembled a wide variety of resource boxes for child-led activities, perhaps this is a good point in the year to ask the children to help you plan which boxes are available for each session?

With the theme of new growth forefront you may want to consider 'resting' part of your forest school area. Some patches will have been used to the extent that they are muddy and wet. With continued use new grass and flowers will struggle to establish themselves. Allowing an area to be free of little feet for a few weeks will pay dividends and the changes will be rapid.

With such a fickle climate in the UK, planning activities that rely on the onset of spring may prove tricky, so there will need to be allowances for the weather and the rate at which we move from winter to spring.

The following set of activities are built around spring proceeding as we would expect. Any snaps of cold weather will put a halt to this new growth and therefore activities may have to be adapted.

Observing and recording

Objectives

- To learn the observational skills of looking, comparing and recording.
- To share their findings in a variety of ways.

Adult initiated ideas

Lead a walk around the forest school area, challenging each child to find one thing they can show others. Stop periodically to discuss the things children are finding, reinforce that we shouldn't pick anything because it stops its growth. Show the children how to use the camera to record their findings.

Follow the group walk with time for the children to explore freely, using a camera or paper and pencils to record anything they believe is there because springtime is coming.

Back in the settings help the children to gather their recordings and create a spring-time scrapbook. Have you considered adding pictures to an online blog or your website to keep parents up to date?

The scrap book can be added to over the coming weeks to show how quickly everything is growing. Using some identification charts will help the children find out what they are watching. They might find daffodils, snowdrops, new grass, buds on trees, new leaves on the hedges or tree blossoms. They may also find an increasingly wider selection of mini-beasts, nesting birds and evidence of other wildlife.

Children enjoy making their own records of the development of the seasons.

Using identification charts helps the children to begin to learn more about the native plants they find. www.naturedetectives.org has a range of printable resources for all the seasons.

Exploring what makes seeds grow

Objectives

- To know that most plants are grown from seeds and that seeds come from the plants when they are fully grown.
- To know that seeds need certain conditions to help them grow.
- To begin to take some responsibility for their surroundings.

Adult initiated ideas

This activity can be part of a much wider topic that ranges between indoor and outdoor play. There are many books that support how seeds grow and it would be useful to share a selection of these with the children during the topic.

Many settings are starting to see the benefits of encouraging children to grow plants for themselves; it would appear to be particularly successful if the end result can be eaten!

Before beginning to plant seeds consider where they will be grown and planted out. Do you want flowers, vegetables or some of each? Have you included a mix of seeds that grow quickly and slowly?

We started by planting some cress in empty egg shells, lined with kitchen towels. The children were thrilled to see their seeds growing into plants and enjoyed adding the cress to their snack-time sandwiches. Following this success the children were keen to plant more vegetables and they provided the ideas for their favourite ones: beans, peas, sweetcorn, tomatoes and carrots. I added potatoes to the list, to provide a different kind of seed to examine before planting, and radishes, because I know these grow quite quickly.

We planted and kept the seeds inside until the warmer weather, at which time the children started taking them outside every day for some fresh air. We are fortunate to have a greenhouse that we could use to carry on the growth outside. A simple rota ensured all the children who wanted to were able to water the plants regularly.

The children were surprised how quickly the bean seeds grew inside the classroom.

Planting seeds teaches the children some patience. They begin to understand that sometimes results can't be instant.

Planting potatoes is always rewarding. The children enjoy harvesting, cooking and eating the end results.

Growing a garden

Objectives

- To grow a garden.
- To learn about caring for plants and seedlings.
- To know that in the springtime many plants begin new life.

Adult initiated ideas

The children had shown in the previous sessions that they were keen to grow flowers, so we were able to use this as a starting point for this activity. We talked about what our gardens looked like in the winter and how they were looking now. Several children had noticed that the grass was getting longer, one child even commenting that it made her trousers wet when she played in it.

Use a small seed tray to make a simple garden by sowing grass seeds all over it. The seeds grow quickly if the garden is left inside and soon it will be a bed of green grass. The children can then add some small plug plants of spring bedding and water it daily. Provide some other additions for the children to add: small stones, a container with which to make a pond, some small fences and some chickens borrowed from the farm set. They can also cut the grass as it gets longer.

We took this activity a step further by providing an opportunity for all children to make their own growing model.

Children were excited to be planting their own mini gardens.

When the grass had grown we added it to the farm resources and the children were able to graze animals in their gardens.

Finding out about roots

> **Objectives**
>
> - To know that most plants have roots.
> - To know that plants drink their water through the roots.
> - To begin to understand that we can eat different parts of the plants.

Adult initiated ideas

Several experiments can be carried out that demonstrate that plants have roots.

Add mung beans to a jam jar, these will provide quick and interesting results that can be viewed through the jar. Then of course, they can be eaten as well!

Plant carrot or radish seeds in a transparent container – we used a wormery. The children can watch the roots growing downwards and observe them as they turn into a vegetable that can be harvested and eaten.

Plant potatoes in a potato bag, old dustbin or stack of old tyres. As the green shoots appear cover them with soil, repeat this until the container is full. The potatoes are ready to harvest when the flowers die back. The children are fascinated that the leaves keep growing up towards the light. If you are careful and turn the whole container out the children will see how the potatoes grow in the roots.

Transferring compost into smaller buckets enables the children to reach and apply it more easily.

Planting seeds in clear plastic cups meant the children were able to watch the roots growing.

Child initiated ideas

- Provide a tray full of root vegetables with the roots and foliage still attached. Add magnifying glasses, paper and pencils and examples of drawings of the vegetables.
- Put a bucket of small trowels and forks by an overgrown flowerbed or patch of undergrowth. Encourage the children to weed the area, collecting plants and roots to look at later.
- Add a selection of seeds to a collage area.
- Send the children off to explore the outdoor area looking for seed heads. Collect them in a paper bag and take back to dry out or plant.
- Create a digging space, add trowels, seeds, plant labels and a watering can.

RESOURCES

Adult initiated ideas:

- Forest school kit bag
- Forest school drinks
- Fully charged digital cameras and spare batteries
- Paper, pencils and clipboards
- Spring plant identification charts
- Fiction books about growing seeds (see below)
- A wide variety of seeds, seed trays, compost and plant labels
- Cress seeds, egg boxes and paper towels
- Making a tray garden: large gravel tray, compost, grass seed, plug plants, gravel, small dish for pond etc.
- Mung bean seeds, glass jar
- Clear container, carrot, radish and spring onion seeds, compost
- Seed potatoes, potato grow bags, compost
- Small watering cans

Child initiated ideas:

- Root vegetables, still with roots, magnifying glasses, paper, and pencils
- Trowels and forks
- Selection of seeds, collage area with paper, glue, double-sided tape
- Small paper bags for collecting seeds
- A digging space: old tubs, tyres filled with soil, old sand trays, spades and forks

Useful books:

- *The Tiny Seed* by Eric Carle (Puffin, New Educational Edition 1997)
- *A Seed in Need* by Sam Godwin (Wayland 1998)
- *Jasper's Beanstalk* by Nick Butterworth and Mick Inkpen (Hodder Children's Books 2008)

Case study

We started this series of lessons with a walk around the outdoor classroom. This is quite a frequent event and changes to the environment are discussed and recorded in a variety of ways. On this occasion I was reminded how much we take for granted children's basic understanding of their world. One of the children noticed the sticky buds on the conker tree and wanted to know what they were. We are all guilty of assuming children would know that leaves come from buds, but I thought I'd check. A quick ask around established that in my group of eight five-year-olds only one knew it was the leaves. Other answers included conkers, roots, more sticks and insects! There was a general look of disbelief as I started to explain that the leaves are very scrunched up and unfold when the bud opened.

This event set off a chain of other ideas into motion and we decided that we should watch the leaves unfolding. A suitable branch with sticky buds was chosen and the 'day 1' photo was duly taken. We maintained this daily photo for several weeks until the leaves had unfolded and then the children watched in amazement as the horse chestnut flowers appeared and eventually died back and were replaced with tiny conkers.

The horse chestnut tree is a valuable addition to our site and for so long we had all made the assumption that children knew the leaves were in the buds. It was a learning experience for everyone!

Monitoring the development of the buds helped the children to understand where the flowers and leaves on trees come from.

Monthly blog

The most valuable lesson to take from this series of planning is not to make assumptions, as described in the case study. Many children do know, understand and recognise little aspects of their own world, many however do not. Once again it was the unplanned experiences that turned into the most valuable lessons for us all.

It is also worth pointing out that planting with children, whilst it has very valuable learning opportunities, is also very time-consuming. I come across many people who like the idea of planting, but find that the maintenance over the growing period takes up too much time and is often forgotten and the plants don't succeed.

We get around this by allocating 'watering can days' to small groups of children. For this day they water, weed, replant and harvest as necessary. It clearly does need an adult to supervise, but as the children get more experiences the adult role becomes less crucial and the children become virtually independent in their plant care.

If you don't think you can manage the after-care then you could consider sending plants home, but then you wonder how many go on to survive! In the past I have asked parents to come a bit early and support with the plant care on a rota basis; this has worked well and spreads the workload, whilst still involving the children.

However challenging planting in your setting may be, it is well worth the time and trouble.

The potatoes grew well alongside the plastic bottle greenhouse and were watered on a rota basis so that all children had contributed.

Some of the children made Grassheads and were excited to be able to give them a haircut!

Getting parents involved in forest school

One of the fundamental purposes of forest school is to build children's confidence, self-esteem and independence in a challenging, but exciting space. For this to happen the children need to feel comfortable and secure, and in turn, for this to take place, they need to know they have the approval of all the people around them, including their own parents. If a child feels that their family aren't convinced about the benefits of outdoor learning then it is likely the child him/herself will be unsure. Likewise, if the parent is concerned their child will get wet, cold and muddy then the child too will be worried.

To overcome this chain of negativity or, better still, to prevent it starting, parents should be included from the beginning. We do this by running an annual workshop for new parents and carers, during which we introduce them to the benefits of outdoor play, allow them to explore with their child, take a few risks and hear about our strict rules for safety. These workshops take place in all weathers in order to prepare everyone involved for what is ahead. Indeed, some workshops have been in torrential rain, others in temperatures below freezing and some in warm sunshine. It is rare to hear the children complaining about the conditions and although there will always be adults who do not enjoy the outdoors, the vast majority accept that their children do.

Some parents enjoy the concept so much that they offer to come in and help on a regular basis. As with all parent volunteers, they are only allowed to join us if their child is not hindered by their presence. Usually, even if the first couple of sessions are difficult, parent and child find their own approach to make it work for them both.

Keeping parents involved throughout the year is achieved through blog updates, website posts and classroom displays. Weekly notes and photos go home detailing the fun we have had and parents are often asked to help their child continue with similar activities and discussions at home. We have found that over the year a good parent partnership is crucial to successful forest school.

TO DO

- Check your outdoor area again. Things are beginning to grow and whilst elements of the natural world are desired, brambles that stretch across pathways are a hindrance. Cut back rapidly growing undergrowth to keep it manageable.

- Build some new semi-permanent dens using a range of materials: branches and sticks, rope and tarpaulin. Create some that need to be crawled into, some which the children can develop, and a tepee.

- Set up spring resource boxes, specific to your planned activities and learning.

April at forest school

Spring should now be in full swing and the changes that were being monitored in March are rapid now. Keep up the photo book started last month, but make sure the children are still having an input into this. Is there somewhere you can display it in your setting to allow parents to share it with their children? Perhaps parts of it can be added to your website or blog pages?

As with many of the activities we plan for, outside weather plays an important part and April presents a whole set of challenges brought about by our climate. Many of our planned activities relate to the changeable spring weather in the UK and for this reason contingency plans need to be put into place if the weather doesn't oblige! In my experience it rarely does!

Now is a good time to set out some simple observation squares. Mark out a space approximately a metre square using either rope or sticks. Fix them down firmly so that the area remains the same. Using a digital camera record how the square looks now. Over a period of several weeks take more photos that mark the changes and gather them in a timeline for the children to examine.

If you have an area that you could turn into a wild flower meadow begin to think about how it could develop. Wild flowers take some time to become established from seeds, but they are available to buy as small plants and many will grow rapidly. Alternatively ask your parents if they have weeds that they could dig up and add to your meadow. Ensure the grassy patch is left unmown and begin to plant small wild flower plants randomly. With the children plant some seeds that are more guaranteed to grow. Poppies and cornflowers make a colourful addition and can be planted into small pots and cared for before planting out or planted directly into the ground.

Sending home exact details of what help you need usually promotes a good response. I detailed the types of plants we were looking for in our wild flower meadow.

Staying dry

Objectives

- To begin to know how we can keep ourselves dry when we play outside.
- To know how to prepare independently for a rainy day.

Adult initiated ideas

Prepare a box of outdoor clothing that includes rain gear and boots, as well as some less suitable attire. Allow the children to dress themselves for the rain, hopefully they will make the right choices. Encourage them to think about how they will stay warm and dry. What do they wear when they play outside at home or go to the beach on a wet day?

Take the children outside to test their choices (it would be a good idea to make sure all the children have a dry set of clothes to change back into if they need to). Find some puddles to jump and play in, float some boats on the water, explore which things float and sink; supply sieves, watering cans and buckets to encourage the children to play in the puddles. Mark the edges of the puddles to see if the puddle is getting smaller.

At the end of the session ask the children to say whether they got wet. Which parts of them got wet? Do they know why? Often children's feet get wet because the water goes over the top of the boots; could they have stopped that happening?

On returning to the setting make sure all the children change into warm dry clothes.

After a particularly wet month the ditches in the school field were full of water, adding a new dimension to the learning taking place.

Exploring materials

Objectives

- To explore the properties of different materials.
- To establish which materials will keep them dry in the rain.
- To build a shelter that will keep them dry in the rain.

Adult initiated ideas

Give the children plenty of time to explore the dens that you already have in the outdoor area. Find out which are their favourite ones and why. Do they know which den would keep them dry? Can they explain why they believe that?

Supply a box full of sheets of material of differing types: fabric, tarpaulin, net curtains, camouflage netting etc., and some pegs, rope and elastic bands. Provide another box full of pairs of animals. Teach the children the song, 'The animals came in two by two' and talk about how we could get the animals out of the rain.

Explain to the children that they can choose whatever they want to build a den for some of the animals. Give the children the support and time they need, talking about how they can fix their den together, why they think it will stay dry etc.

This activity is best carried out on a rainy day because the children will see immediately what keeps their animals dry and what doesn't. However, if it is not raining how about pouring some water onto the den from a watering can and watching the outcome?

Noah was keen to find a home that would keep his bear dry. After some unsuccessful attempts with some cardboard boxes, Noah discovered that an upturned bucket keeps the water out.

Where do mini-beasts live?

> **Objectives**
>
> - To consider where mini-beasts live.
> - To establish whether mini-beasts prefer dry or damp conditions.
> - To identify a few common mini-beasts and know where to find them.

Adult initiated ideas

Provide the children with a range of hunting equipment. Children enjoy taking on a role to play; perhaps they could be dressed as hunters, with hats and camouflage clothing? Help the children identify any insects they find using a simple ID chart. Gather a few in a suitable container to observe later.

Gather the children back together to discuss what they have found and where it was? There will probably be a pattern underneath a log or stone. Talk about how it must feel to live in such a place. Encourage and explain the use of the words 'dark', 'damp', 'quiet', etc.

Give the children magnifying glasses to examine the collected mini-beasts. Make sure all the mini-beasts are returned to the same place they were gathered from.

Make a home for a few woodlice. Ask the children to make suggestions about what it should be like. Deliberately make part of the home, perhaps in a shoe box, dark and damp with lots of hiding places. Leave the other part dry and uncovered. Can the children monitor where the woodlice are going? Perhaps set up a counting jar, adding a pebble to it if the woodlice come to the dry end. Add another jar at the dark end and repeat. Which jar has the most pebbles? Once again return the woodlice to their preferred environment.

The children were experts at finding mini-beasts!

But catching them was a bit trickier!

Making an umbrella

> **Objectives**
>
> - To use existing knowledge about waterproof materials to make their own umbrellas.
> - To explore methods of fixing different materials.

Adult initiated ideas

Reuse your box of different materials for this activity. Children can either bring their own or use a spare umbrella during this session. Depending on the age of the children you may need to have a short discussion about safety and umbrella use! Provide a range of umbrellas in different sizes, with different handles and patterns on.

After the children have had a chance to explore their umbrella, show them some 'broken' ones that have no covers on them. Suggest that they help you make them again using the materials from the box.

The children should have a better understanding of what constitutes waterproof and will be able to select some suitable fabric for covering. For this activity the children will probably need an adult close by to ask for help with cutting and fixing the fabric. However, let the children work out how they can make the umbrella waterproof again by attaching their fabric to the open frame, only intervening if they ask you to or at the point when their interest is waning.

Some efforts will probably not be very successful, but the children will persevere and with a helping hand should be able to find a secure way of fixing everything together.

Back at the setting the umbrella theme could continue with a large sports umbrella. Gather some colourful plastic bags and cut them open so they are flat. These can be cut into strips and woven around the prongs to create a unique waterproof brolly for your outside area.

Child initiated ideas

- Create a resource box of waterproof and non-waterproof materials, small watering cans and bottles of water.
- Make a 'Puddle Bucket'. Add boats and other floating objects, sieves, a small watering can and some chunky paintbrushes for water painting.
- Ask the children to help you put together a mini-beast hunting box. Include hunting clothing, magnifying glasses, collection pots, ID charts and small trowels or spades.
- Make a basket of small-world play toys, including dolls and their clothing, suitable for wet days.

RESOURCES

Adult initiated ideas:

- Large quantity of outdoor clothing and footwear
- Box of materials, some of them waterproof. Fixing kit: clothes pegs, pipe cleaners, elastic bands, string and rope
- Hunter box, appropriate clothing, magnifying glasses, mini-beast ID charts
- Shoebox for mini-beast experiment, with gravel, pebbles, moss, soil, sand, wet and dry leaves. Cut the lid in half so that one end stays dark
- Glass jars and pebbles
- Variety of umbrellas, different sizes and designs, some of them broken
- Large collection of coloured plastic bags for making umbrellas

Child initiated ideas:

- Materials resource box
- Hunter box
- Puddle bucket
- Basket of dolls, teddies etc., and their clothing

Case study

We had spent a lot of time outside enjoying the rainy weather and the puddles in the lead-up to this set of lessons, so the children were entirely sure of the clothing they needed to collect from the basket before they went outside. They were less sure of the materials that would keep the rain out of their dens though, so this became the main focus.

After an initial session where the children were clearly confused about what they were being asked to do I reassessed how we approached the next session. We took the same objectives but started the session slightly differently on this occasion. Before leaving the setting each child was asked to collect a small soft toy to take with them. We added a collection of junk boxes and containers to the resources for that day. The children's remit was to build a house for their toy which helped keep it dry. Having had so many wet sessions, this one was of course a dry day so we also took bottles of water and a watering can. The children grasped this much quicker than building their own shelter and set to work exploring in which containers their toys would be safe.

One child, the youngest in the group, was adamant that his cereal box was a good shelter and proceeded to stuff his bear inside along with some leaves to keep him warm. He didn't want to use the watering can and instead put the box, and teddy, straight into a puddle. He wasn't at all concerned that the box sank, and when he fished it back out he told me that teddy would be dry. He tipped his bear out and teddy was indeed dry! I suggested he tried again with something else, but he was determined that teddy liked his box and repeatedly put the bear in and out of the box and the puddle. The first few occasions teddy did stay dry, but on the fourth go teddy got very wet as the cereal box completely collapsed. The boy took the bear out and handed him to me saying, 'washing line'. Together we hung the bear on our outdoor line and returned to the junk. The boy selected another box and a spare teddy. He spent the next twenty five minutes repeating the exploration, several more toys were added to the washing line before the boy said, 'my turn'. He proceeded to jump into the middle of the puddle and wade around. As we left the area he told another member of staff that the wet teddies should have had wellies to keep their feet dry. We were able to note that he had realised his boots were made of a material that had kept him dry.

Wet teddies were hung on the line to drip dry!

Monthly blog

Over the period of about two months our puddle bucket developed into a resource that was used on an everyday basis, both in the playground and the outdoor classroom. Various items were added to it to keep it changing and the children began bringing things from home to include as well. It included decorating rollers and brushes, washing-up liquid, mirrors, sponges, stretches of the marble run to act as guttering, plant sprayers, watering cans, various receptacles and spoons of various sizes and a selection of floating and sinking natural materials.

The learning that came from such a simple collection of everyday items extended far beyond the original objectives and the children quickly generated their own experiments and activities.

The bucket provided numerous ways for a few children to explore their trajectory schema with a variety of ways to watch running water. They were secure in their choice of activity and always made sure they were well dressed for the weather, without our intervention.

Rather interestingly we also noticed a lot less play taking place in the cloakrooms around the taps and sinks!

9 May

Bringing the outdoors in

Outdoor play is exciting, provides new experiences and plenty of time and space for child-initiated play, but however much we believe in the outdoor lifestyle there are times when the children need to be inside, or at least have that choice.

Children in the Foundation Stage, particularly those in a school environment, are often given limits to their play: how long they can have, where they can go or which toys they can access. This timetabled learning interferes with a child's opportunity to enter deep-level uninterrupted play experiences. This is especially true in the context of a forest school, where time allocated is often limited.

To overcome this, early years providers should make allowances and plan for outdoor experiences to be modified and continued indoors. For example, there is often a sand tray outside and a similar set up inside so the children can continue their exploring when the outside resource becomes unavailable to them. This should be true of forest school experiences as well.

To bring the outside in requires just a little additional planning and resource collecting. For example, this month we are talking about using natural materials to make two- and three-dimensional art. By adding this to the indoor planning as well children can finish what they have started or try a new approach.

It can be achieved by dedicating a space in the classroom to forest school-style play, providing resources that support the outdoor planning and allowing the children to fetch additional items as they require. A well-equipped indoor forest school area will have accessible baskets of natural items, pictures and photos of outdoor play, and a range of identification charts and pictures. It should have an active area as well, perhaps a tray of compost or soil, an interactive table of seasonal items, toys made from natural materials and maybe the space to do some indoor den building.

TO DO

- Check the children have the appropriate clothing and footwear, weather conditions are changing and getting warmer. The children should still have long-sleeved tops and long trousers.

- Do some maintenance on the forest school kit bag – is it still complete, does anything need replacing?

- Update parents about the changing hazards in your area, such as insect bites and stings, rapid growing brambles and nettles. Ensure they have provided you with the correct medical details.

- Invite parents and family members to look at the changing displays and photos taken at forest school.

May at forest school

As it does so often, the weather will be playing an important part in your forest school sessions. Whilst the nights and the mornings can still be quite cold, the daytime temperatures are starting to creep up. As adults we take this in our stride, but children need a bit more guidance. They will be excited to be outside, they will not necessarily know the risks of too much sun so a key role for early years workers during the summer months is to be vigilant. Prepare your parents for the extras they will need to supply: hats, water bottles and suncream (check your settings policy on applying suncream first).

The activities planned for this month can be done at any time, some of them are more specific to the warmer weather and a time of growing, but others can be done when it suits your group of children. We use these as part of a big topic about art and creativity using different mediums and environments. You can be as creative as you like. I use the work of Andy Goldsworthy as inspiration, but maybe you have a local artist or sculptor who can visit and provide first-hand ideas and excitement.

Natural art

Objectives

- To use natural resources to create unique artwork.
- To recognise art as individual and to know that others share differing opinions.
- To explore colour, texture, pattern and shape in their environment.

Adult initiated ideas

Talk to the children about colour in their world. Discuss the things you can see around you. Are they the same if you walk to another area? Using some large laminated pictures of the artwork by Andy Goldsworthy, begin a discussion about shape and pattern. What materials does this artist use to make his pictures? You will be able to find examples of his work that use stones, leaves, sticks and other natural materials.

Choose a few examples of this style of artwork and encourage the children to consider what natural materials they can gather to make their own pictures.

Allow the children to take photos to display alongside the work that was the inspiration.

Daisies are prolific in most school fields and make a really easy way of recreating some natural artwork.

One of the girls followed up some work we had been doing about pattern using the flowers and leaves around her.

Stick art

Objectives

- To consider how natural materials can be used in their work.
- To show creativity through their approach to something new.
- To sort materials according to common features: length, shape, colour.

Adult initiated ideas

In this session we continued to be inspired by the work of Andy Goldsworthy. We had been learning about two- and three-dimensional shapes in the setting so we brought that learning outside.

Ask the children to collect as many sticks as they can find, even from the firewood pile because they can still be reused. Encourage the children to collect the sticks according to size and length. Are there any other materials they would like to use? Small pebbles, gravel, fir-cones etc.

Discuss the kind of art the children can make with the sticks: nests, fires and small dens.

Give the children the freedom to create independently, encouraging collaboration and sharing.

Take photos to share back in the setting.

This boy used his sticks to make a 'fire', using the cross hatch method that we often used for fire lighting.

Some of our stick sculptures were added to over several weeks. Similar structures can also be built around tree trunks.

These two boys had very firm ideas about what they were building. When they had finished they told me it was a house!

Storybook pictures

Objectives

- To relate their independent work to a familiar theme and share their ideas with those around them.
- To show pride in their work, helping to display and show off their ideas.

Adult initiated ideas

If you have been working on a particular story this could be the basis for this activity. Themes such as 'The Three Little Pigs', 'The Billy Goats Gruff' and 'Little Red Riding Hood' work well because they contain familiar characters and settings.

Give the children small baskets to collect natural materials. They could work in pairs, but this activity often works better if the children work on their own.

When they have gathered their collage material explain that they can use them to make pictures of whatever they want. Guide them towards a theme if you feel you need to, for example a picture of the little pigs house or the Billy Goats' bridge.

To encourage improved communication skills ask the children to explain to their friends or an adult what their picture is about. Can they describe it? How many doors and windows or added features does it have?

Take some photos and in the setting ask the children to label the printed pictures.

Both these pictures represent the story of 'The Three Little Pigs'.

Natural mobiles

Objectives

- To show independence in thought and practical approach.
- To make links in their learning to previous sessions.
- To work successfully with others, asking for help when it is needed.

Adult initiated ideas

Remind the children about the work they have been doing by sharing photos from the previous sessions.

Explain that in this session we are going to decorate the outdoor classroom using the things we can find on the floor.

Tie up a long washing line and ask the children to add things to it.

Supply a box of string and scissors and give the children the time to work with others to make hanging decorations.

Tying string at such a young age is tricky for most children. If you want the children to succeed without adult support consider adding pipe cleaners to the box so that the children can fix them on their own. However, it can also be beneficial to work with the children showing them how to tie their own simple knot.

Celebrate the successes and talk about the difficulties.

Once the children know they can tie things together and hang them on the line they will often return to this activity independently.

The hanging mobiles can be made a little more elaborate when children work with each other or an adult.

Child initiated ideas

The children are becoming far more comfortable in the outdoor area now and the need to provide resources for free play is slightly reduced. The children have a large bank of ideas to draw upon based on previous visits and can quite easily entertain themselves. But to ensure learning and development keep the resources changing and consider how you develop their play further.

Set up a 'Tie it Together' resource box containing string, rope, elastic bands, pipe cleaners, sticky-tape and scissors.

Add new resources to the collage box: pressed flowers and leaves, sea shells, small pebbles and wooden beads and buttons.

Make a book of pictures that inspire art in the outdoors, laminate it and allow the children time to look at it. Perhaps set the books and some additional pictures up inside a den with blankets and cushions.

RESOURCES

Adult initiated ideas:

- Forest school kit bag
- Forest school drinks
- Large, colour, laminated copies of artwork by Andy Goldsworthy

- Digital cameras and spare batteries
- A selection of natural materials; some will be readily available; others may need to be brought to the setting
- Small baskets for collecting items
- String, rope, pipe cleaners, elastic bands and scissors

Child initiated ideas:

- The 'Tie it Together' box (string, rope, scissors, elastic bands, pipe cleaners, pegs and wire hooks for hanging)
- Collage box, with a few new added items (pressed flowers, leaves, shells, wooden beads and buttons)
- Book of laminated pictures, showing art inspired by nature

Useful books:

- *Natural: Simple Land Art through the Seasons* by Marc Pouyet (Frances Lincoln 2009)
- *Wood: Andy Goldsworthy* by Andy Goldsworthy (Thames and Hudson 2010)

Case study

As anyone who has worked with young children knows, children, string and tying knots frequently go together, but rarely in a particularly successful way. We provide lots of string and opportunities to tie things together, with the knowledge that we will have to surreptitiously re-tie the objects if the children are to succeed. However, children persevere and this is always a popular pastime.

For these activities, string was provided throughout all the sessions for free play experiences. During the first session, little bundles of sticks were wrapped together, just to fall apart when the child tried to move them. This child persevered and repeatedly picked up the sticks, wrapped string around and carried them to the log circle to share. Each time the bundle fell to pieces, but he never came to ask for help or appeared frustrated.

In the next session I had added elastic bands to the resource box. The same child repeated his activities of the week before; gathering sticks, wrapping them in string and then putting the loosely tied bundle by the fire. He did look in the box and pulled out a handful of elastic bands, before taking the string and scissors. It didn't feel right to interfere at this stage.

For the third session the box had string and scissors, elastic bands and pipe cleaners. The same child busied himself making stick bundles. The string, as on other visits unravelled and the bundles were small piles of sticks, with string across them. After the first two or three bundles the boy stopped to examine the pipe cleaners. He bent them several times and then wrapped one around his finger. From this he wrapped one around some sticks. His bundle really was a bundle on this occasion and the joy on his face when he realised he had succeeded was indescribable.

Monthly blog

We currently have an extensive outdoor classroom that involves all children and staff visiting together for a specific, limited amount of time. We also have an outdoor area alongside the indoor setting that adds a different dimension to outdoor play and is usually a free-flow environment giving children a choice of places to play.

We also work hard to find ways in our planning and classroom layout that bring the outside in. This allows the children the opportunity to continue their line of enquiry at other times, it takes some of the weather limitations out of the equation and provides us with an area for showing off what we have achieved outside. This is particularly true through this set of sessions, where the many photos became a focal point in the setting.

We have an outdoor classroom rule that we don't pick things that are growing, but on this occasion we discussed which flowers we felt we could use. One of the children had already noticed that however many daisies she picked at home for daisy chains there were always lots more. This led us to agree that we could pick daisies because they were so prolific. A similar conversation took place about dandelions with a different child knowing that there were always lots of flowers to pick for her guinea pig. It's always lovely when the children can relate what you are doing to something that is familiar and normal in their own lives.

We had agreed prior to this set of activities that picking and using daisies was acceptable.

Using children's individual learning patterns at forest school

One of the successes of the forest school approach is that it allows for the opportunity to be flexible in your planning, making more allowances for children's individual learning styles and behaviours. The environment itself is ever changing and usually large enough to allow for more freedom than is available in the majority of settings.

Recognising children's preferred method of learning ensures their views, play and learning are valued and that they receive the praise and approval they are often seeking. Making good use of your observations from indoors makes sure you plan for outdoor experiences that will interest your children. For example, if you have recognised that someone in your care is working within the transporting schema then ensure that you supply a collection of bags, boxes and trolleys for your forest school sessions. They will find their own way of using them to continue their exploration. However, if you specifically want them to get involved in your activity then provide the resources that will inspire them to be interested. Can they collect the resources from the shed, gather sticks in a large shopping bag or be responsible for handing round the cups?

One of the things that appeal to many practitioners is that forest school can be more free-flow than many settings are able to be. This enables children to engage in deep-level learning experiences where they can stay and explore for as long as their interest is held. It is important to provide for this as much as possible. We usually have a whole group drink and snack time, but with the flexibility for children to drop in and out if they prefer. How can you manage this in your environment?

Children learn predominantly through hands-on, practical approaches; there is very little that can beat forest school when it comes to this provision. Whether your children are visual, auditory or kinaesthetic learners your session will automatically be making allowances for this. With the freedom to opt in and out of adult-led experiences the children will be able to learn in a way, and at a pace, that suits them as individual people.

This particular boy learnt in a very practical and physical way. In the outdoor classroom he kept himself out of trouble and achieved really well over the year.

TO DO

- Update staff training, reminding everyone about managed risk, the outdoor classroom rules and behaviour expectations. This is a good opportunity to ensure everyone is applying the same approach and positive attitude. Make sure it is a two way communication and that others viewpoints are taken seriously.

- Take a little time to look at how praise and encouragement is managed. Has anyone found something that is working particularly well and can it be shared and adopted by others?

- Have a close scrutiny of the assessment taking place. What trends are there? Is there anyone who is consistently missed off the observations? If so how can this be rectified?

- Begin to consider any end-of-year celebration you might want to involve parents in.

June at forest school

If your climate is following the norm for the UK, this is the month when everything will suddenly grow. You may well find that you don't visit forest school for a week, perhaps because of half term, and when you do the path has disappeared under the brambles, nettles and other rapidly growing undergrowth.

Ensure you have prepared for this and made arrangements for your grounds maintenance people to be available when you need them. If you take this aspect of your area into your own remit, make some plans for other people to help. Often parents are quite happy to turn out for a couple of hours on a Saturday morning to support with an annual clear up.

Don't make the mistake of cutting everything back. If you take away all the nettles you also remove the busiest ladybird homes; if you cut back all the brambles there will be no blackberries to pick in the autumn. I also believe children need to learn to negotiate these everyday plants with their stings and thorns.

The weather is improving now; the sun is warmer and the shade under the trees is very welcome on warm afternoons. Utilise it and enjoy it as much as possible.

This month's planning takes full advantage of the leafy green trees and the wild flowers that are now in abundance.

Summer colours

Objectives

- To use the new growth to create pictures.
- To know some of the names of simple flowers and be aware of which ones they can pick.
- To begin to understand there are many shades of one colour.

Adult initiated ideas

This is an activity that can be carried out throughout the year. The results will always be varied and will chart the difference in the seasons.

Gather together some laminated cards in different colours. You could choose shades of colours the children will definitely find in your outdoor area, or to challenge the children you can add some random colours they are less likely to find.

Each child chooses a card from the box and has to find as many things as they can in that colour.

On this occasion I added pale pink, white, green and yellow, reflecting the colours of the wild flowers I was happy to let the children pick.

Provide a range of paper in different shapes and sizes, some glue sticks and double-sided tape. The children can choose how they fix their finds, and whether to make a picture, pattern or individual art. Cutting some of the paper into strips allows the children to make crowns or wristbands if they want.

Do the children know the name of the flowers from which they are collecting their petals and leaves? Do they recognise that one colour has many shades and have they noticed that all the petals from the same flower are slightly different?

Clearly this child had enjoyed his session outside, achieving a great deal and able to tell me what he had found for his crown.

These girls spent a long time looking for flower petals in the long undergrowth.

Not wanting to pick any flowers or petals, this little girl had chosen to make her crown mostly using green leaves.

Leafy green pictures

Objectives

- To use a selection of leaves, recognising that each tree grows a different shape leaf.
- To be creative in their work, talking about their actions and process.
- To share their results in a small group of people, talking with clarity and confidence.

Adult initiated ideas

Ask the children to look at the trees in your outdoor area. What do they notice? Discuss their ideas.

Put out a selection of leaves, already gathered. Can the children find the trees they came from?

Show the children how they can use the leaves to make a picture.

When the children have finished ask them to share their picture, talking about what it is and why they chose that subject.

These two pictures show different trees in the outdoor classroom. They were described by the child as 'a tall tree with lots of leaves and another tree without lots of leaves!'

Exploring camouflage

> **Objectives**
>
> - To begin to understand how birds and animals stay hidden.
> - To use the materials around them to hide successfully.

Adult initiated ideas

Show the children pictures of camouflaged birds and animals. What do they notice about them? Can they find the hiding creature easily? Why not?

Explain that we are going to play hide and seek and the children have to make sure they are not discovered too quickly.

Provide a large quantity of leafy undergrowth, some string and scissors. We also added elastic bands so the children could be more independent.

Encourage the children to consider finding their own greenery to add to your own. Which bits of their body will we see easily? Look at pictures of children who have played this game before, explain that they have also put something on their faces to help them blend in more.

Add a box of charcoal to the branches. What else could we use?

Some of the children may be reluctant to smear mud or charcoal on their faces and hands, but they are usually very happy putting it onto one of their carers! Often, if they are able to do this, they are happier to add it to themselves afterwards. They should not be made to feel they have to do this though; it should be their own decision.

Play hide and seek. During the snack break talk about the things that gave the children away: noise, movement, brightly coloured clothes etc.

Covered in undergrowth and with charcoal on their faces, the children played hide and seek for most of the session. They truly believed they were invisible!

Making a bird hide

Objectives

- To use the material around them to make a natural panel that will act as a bird hide.
- To choose materials from the outdoor area that will blend in.
- To weave the chosen materials and fix securely.

Adult initiated ideas

Depending on how long you have you can either make a panel using horizontal and vertical sticks tied together, or you can have one or more pre-made.

Discuss how the children made themselves camouflaged in the previous session. How can they use that knowledge to make the panel blend in?

Give the children safety scissors and remind them how to move around with them. Most of the children should be able to cut through some undergrowth to weave into the panels.

Show the children how to thread their branches through the sticks, but allow them to do their own. It doesn't really matter if the branches aren't tightly fixed.

When the panels are covered, secure them to upright posts or trees. These can become semi-permanent structures that can be used for multiple activities. We placed ours so that the children could watch the birds coming down to feed.

If the stick structure is strong enough this activity can be repeated throughout the summer with a constantly changing range of materials.

Once the structure had been tied into place the children were shown how to fix their greenery. They were encouraged to be independent and by the end of the session several woven stick panels were well covered, ready for the bird hide.

Child initiated ideas

Over this month as you introduce new ideas they will probably become the children's own choice of activity, the resources and management will be quite simple.

Provide collage paper and glue for children to make their own pieces of natural art work.

Continue to ensure an endless supply of rope, elastic bands, scissors, tarpaulins and blankets.

Change the ID charts to include any birds you have visiting you regularly.

Leave a mini-beast hunting kit to hand.

Make some small stick weaving panels and hang some completed ones in the trees for inspiration.

RESOURCES

Adult initiated ideas:

- Forest school kit bag
- Forest school drinks bag
- Small pieces of coloured and laminated card
- Paper and card in a range of sizes and shapes
- Glue and double-sided tape
- Previously gathered green leaves, from a variety of trees
- Paper and glue
- Scissors or secateurs, for adult use only
- String, elastic bands
- Charcoal (perhaps some you have previously made over the fire?)
- Flasks of warm water and paper towels for washing if necessary
- Sticks of varying lengths to make weaving panel
- String and rope for fixing

Child initiated ideas:

- A collage basket: paper, card, scissors, glue sticks, sticky-tape
- Den building materials: rope, string, tarpaulins, blankets, camouflage nets, fixing pegs
- Identification charts for visiting birds
- Min-beast hunting kit
- Small woven panels, scissors and string. Previously made examples

---

Case study

Marie was a quiet girl who frequently told us she didn't like the outdoor area. She was always dressed cleanly and smartly, and her clothes for outside were also new and pretty. We felt she was becoming rather uncomfortable about spoiling her clothes and approached Mum about providing something more suitable. It transpired from that conversation that Mum didn't like the idea of mud and dirt and as a result didn't really want Marie taking part. She agreed that Marie should go out with her friends, but didn't change the clothing as requested.

On the week we were doing the camouflage activity we lent Marie one of our coats to wear, explaining that her lovely pink coat wasn't going to make it easy for her to hide. She was happy to accept this and came with us.

We saw a marked improvement in Marie that week and she joined in all the activities with enthusiasm, even smearing mud and charcoal on my face before doing her own.

Explaining to Mum what an impact an old coat had made to Marie's attitude resulted in Mum providing an old jumper for Marie to wear. It was becoming too warm for coats now and most children just had an extra jumper, Marie was quite happy with this outcome.

This was a real turning point for Marie and she continued to join in with more and more enthusiasm on each visit. She was still the first to wash her hands on return to the setting, but rarely complained again whilst we were outside.

Monthly blog

This series of activities put some of the focus back on the staff in our setting. It clearly showed those who were willing to take a full and active part, and those who were not. We carried out a short training session together where we looked at the impact our own attitude was having on the children's learning. It was quickly apparent that the staff returning with charcoal and mud on their faces and grass clipped in their hair were having the most impact on their children, and I should add, the most fun!

Some of the adults, quite rightly, didn't want mud smeared on their faces, but were happy to have it on their waterproof trousers or their coat sleeves and it was agreed that this was still taking part and showing the children that it was actually OK to get a bit mucky.

I don't believe any adult should have to do something they are uncomfortable with, but I do think it is our job to make a few sacrifices. We are, after all, there to support the children, to spread enthusiasm and have fun with them.

Hide and seek never seems to be exhausted, as it is played frequently. In this instance the children are happy to be the ones covered in grass and mud while the adult is the finder.

Planning for unexpected learning

One of the undeniable successes of forest school, regardless of the age group with which you are working, is its ability to fit with everyone. The original concept of this style of teaching and learning was that it would be child led, not heavily planned by those leading the session. There is a danger that as forest school becomes more commonplace it also becomes as well-prepared and meticulously delivered as the learning that takes place in classrooms everywhere.

Whilst the planning elements of this publication contradict this approach, it should be noted that practitioners are quite able to, and should, change and adapt during the session to suit the needs of their group and of the individuals within it.

Forest schools and groups accessing this approach need to start somewhere and letting loose a group of five-year-olds in unfamiliar territory without some thought is likely to lead to chaotic learning and even unsafe incidents. It is with this in mind that planning should be used to create some initial learning opportunities.

Setting up for a session should be thorough and well prepared, but with the understanding that children are likely to use the initial ideas to develop their own play. It is with experience and confidence that practitioners can identify the learning taking place, note it, and then ensure it is provided for in alternative ways on following visits.

Once a child or a group of children has the confidence to seek out their own opportunities, planning becomes less crucial, and preparation and resources take a higher precedence. As with all good early years practice allowing the child to seek out their own experiences is likely to result in more deep-level learning experiences that relate to the child's interests and curiosity.

Not all children will show this level of maturity and confidence in this new learning space, so this is when planning becomes more important and the adult working with the child is able to use their own skills to support in the early stages. Children adapt surprisingly quickly and with such sympathetic support even the most unsure five-year-old will begin to develop their skills independently.

Much planning and scribing, for the learning that takes place outside, takes the form of observations and annotations made during the session. Photos are a good source of reference for the provision in later sessions. Each setting will find their own way, but without a copious amount of paperwork that is likely to be cast aside to follow the child in their own exploration.

TO DO

- Whatever type of setting you are working in it is likely that some of your children will be moving on towards the end of this month. Perhaps they are leaving to start school in September or moving to the next year group? This is the time to ensure that all your assessments are up to date and collated into the correct framework for transition.

- Add photos to the child's own photo record and keep the settings planning up to date by ensuring observations, annotations and photos are clearly linked to the curriculum.

- Plan a visit for the children that attend during the school holidays, a day at the seaside, local park or riverside.

- Prepare children for their transition to new settings by helping them recognise the progress they have been making and how they can use their skills to settle somewhere new.

July at forest school

As always, the weather plays an important part in playing outside. July can be very warm and children need to be kept safe from the sun, particularly in the middle of the day. If your sessions involve being out in the hottest part of the day ensure the children bring sun hats and suncream to reapply. There are some very effective suncreams that will last all day if parents would rather you did not apply it yourself. The children and the staff should be wearing long sleeves and long trousers, both to minimise sun exposure and to reduce the risk of stings and bites. Each child should be wearing a hat.

If your session time can be flexible, consider taking the children earlier in the morning when it is cooler. But even then the rules about covering up and suncream should still apply.

Make sure the children have access to cool water throughout the session. At this time of year we stop the hot chocolate treat and provide cold water instead, often with some fresh fruit.

Wherever possible make sure the children have access to shade and water throughout the session.

Pond exploration

Objectives

- To explore the importance of water in our environment.
- To use learnt skills and use identification charts to name some of the local pond life and plants.
- To learn how to use some simple equipment to pond dip.

Adult initiated ideas

Ensure the children have a clear understanding of the safety rules surrounding the pond. We only have six children at the pond at any time and always with an adult. The children need to know how to approach safely and how to remain safe at the water's edge. We start the children off by lying on the ground looking at the surface of the water. If they are older or more confident they can kneel at the edge. When they are ready to leave they back away slowly.

Ponds are full of living things – wildlife and plants – at this time of year. Provide a selection of pond dipping equipment and some identification charts. Do the children know what they might find in the pond? Take some suggestions and then ask the children to explore their theories by looking.

Can they work out what they have caught? How many legs, wings, marking etc. does their mini-beast have? Take photos of the finds to label and display back in the setting. Remind the children to return their finds carefully to the place they found them.

While some of the children are pond dipping others can be looking for some of the plants that are found near water. Do some of the plants look familiar? Where else have the children seen them?

While some of the children were pond dipping others reverted to an activity from a previous session and made some natural art work.

Don't be afraid to introduce printable resources. These life-cycle cards helped the children to understand that the tadpoles they had seen a few weeks earlier were now frogs. (www.sparklebox.co.uk)

A day at the seaside

> **Objectives**
>
> - To make comparisons between the school grounds and the seaside.
> - To have time to explore their surroundings, following their own interest safely.
> - To use the natural resources to extend learning experiences and create new ones.

Adult initiated ideas

Visits off the site require meticulous planning and preparation. Be sure to follow your own health and safety guidelines. Checking the time of high and low water is likely to be crucial to the success of your day out. I always take my groups to a beach that is life-guarded, but if this not an option for you, it is prudent to secure the paid services of a beach lifeguard for the day, regardless of the tide conditions.

Consider whether you want to invite parents to join you, or whether you can manage the legal off-site ratios for your age group without them.

Consider essentials such as toilets, lunch, travel and the presence of the general public in your preparations. Is there anywhere for you to retreat to should it rain? Take the usual forest school kit bags and first-aid as well as emergency phone numbers, plenty of water, dry clothing and if necessary waterproof coats.

Once at the beach, set up a selection of activities for the children to enjoy. They may include sandcastle/sculpture building, rock pooling, scavenger hunting and beach games. These should all be supervised closely and within well marked out areas. Perhaps the children can all wear high visibility vests so you can see them at a glance. All adults working with you should have their own copy of the day's agenda and your emergency phone number.

A sandy beach with nearby water provided this child with lots of opportunities to make 'mixtures'.

A nearby adult changed beachcombing into a fact-finding session.

Even a single piece of driftwood can change the dynamics of the play. This stick was dragged around and covered in sand during our visit.

Finding out about streams and rivers

Objectives

- To use knowledge of the usual forest school setting to make comparisons with a new area.
- To explore using the senses of sight, hearing, touch and feel.
- To investigate the area using some of the skills taught previously.

Adult initiated ideas

This session will involve another visit off the site so you may have to consider the cost implications to the families involved.

On this occasion the session is based on a visit to a local stream or shallow river. It is likely that your off-site resources and risk assessment will be similar to that of the beach visit, but they will need adjusting to suit the group and the conditions, as well as the location of the visit. Once again the children will need to be well-prepared with appropriate clothing and footwear, packed lunch and drinks, dry clothes, spare shoes and a towel.

Provide a selection of pond dipping resources and the identification charts.

Encourage children to try and stop the flow of the water using the natural resources around them. With an adult supporting them, can the children build a bridge over the water.

What can the children find on the river bed?

Provide time before returning to discuss what the children have enjoyed and learnt about. Celebrate any successes and praise the children for their behaviour.

Building a dam in a river is a full-time occupation for this boy.

These children enjoyed exploring the depth of the river. Water running into their welly boots was an essential part of the activity.

Sitting around a pond is a calm and quiet activity. Whilst excited, these children spoke quietly and sat calmly for some time.

Making a habitat for pond creatures

> **Objectives**
>
> - To use knowledge acquired from their local visits to make a new environment.
> - To demonstrate an understanding of what creatures need to survive.
> - To take part in a group activity, providing ideas and listening to others.

Adult initiated ideas

For this activity you can use a small fish tank or bowl. Consider whether using glass is viable or should it be plastic?

Suggest to the children that you are going to make a home for some pond creatures to visit. They will only be staying a short time, but what will they need?

Draw on the information gathered from visits to the pond and river areas to help the children draw up a list of the items you will need to make a pond.

Ask the children to suggest how the items can be gathered and make the necessary visit to the pond to collect them: plants, small stones, large stones and water should be brought back.

When the pond is ready the children can pond dip to find some creatures to live in their pond for the day.

Do they remember the names of any of the things they have found?

Set up an observation area near the 'pond'. This could include pencils, paper, identification pictures and labels, magnifying glasses and a camera.

At the end of the day return all the creatures and plants to their natural habitat.

Child initiated ideas

This month has produced a very different range of activities for the children you look after to experience. Most of the visits provide ample opportunity for children to initiate their own play, but it is likely you will find they want to join you in a range of slightly more structured ideas.

To ensure opportunities for children to be independent, make sure that there is always a basket of familiar items to hand. This could include: rope and string, a shelter cover, paper and pencils, books that relate to your location and a mini beast hunting kit.

RESOURCES

Adult initiated ideas:

- Forest school kit bag
- Forest school drinks bag
- Pond dipping kit: nets of differing lengths and sizes, small white trays, magnifying pots, magnifying glasses, small clear buckets, pond life identification charts
- Local plant identification charts
- Selection of beach toys
- Beach life identification chart

While the rest of the group were enjoying the stream, this child chose to build himself a den.

- Camera and spare batteries
- Small fish tank

Child initiated ideas:

- Rope and string
- Paper and pencils
- Shelter building materials
- Books about the local environment
- Mini-beast hunt kit

Case study

Two of the four-year-olds with us on our visit to a nearby river were notoriously difficult to keep entertained and would often be found pushing the boundaries in their play. They were not bothersome to the other children but were a concern to the staff who felt they needed to be shadowed at all times.

The location we were visiting was a public area. Although rarely used on week days there was some concern that there would be other children playing in the same area. On our arrival it was clear no one else was there and the physical boundaries and rules about staying safe were clearly explained to the children and their understanding was assessed through some simple questions.

The two children of concern listened intently and then at the first opportunity went to the stream area, closely shadowed by a member of staff. For several minutes the boys were content to move stones around and build a dam. But with the arrival of the rest of the group they went further upstream, just within the allocated area, again with a member of staff.

Away from the other children they again settled to build a dam. Once again it was interrupted by some others and the boys wandered off again. It became apparent that they actually had very fixed ideas about what they wanted to do, based on a similar family visit one of them had recently made to the same site.

Having left the stream area the boys were now beginning to get themselves into trouble by throwing sticks and pretending to play 'dogs'. The staff member had identified what the boys had originally wanted to do and quickly cleared it with me for the boys to go to a location a few minutes away, where the other children wouldn't join them. It was agreed two adults should go.

Having some space to themselves the boys once again set about building a dam and entertained themselves for over an hour trying to divert the river.

When they returned to the rest of the group, they were settled and each went off happily to play with a different group of children.

On this occasion, because of the nature of the experience, it was crucial that the children kept within the safe guidelines. Through their initial play both these boys were in danger of hurting themselves and others. It was prevented by a supportive adult and their excitement was successfully channelled into purposeful play.

Building a dam was the sole activity that kept these children happy for an afternoon.

Monthly blog

Looking for wildlife in the pond.

Our visit to the school pond area is something that takes place frequently throughout the year. The children have noticed that there is little to catch when it gets colder and have learnt not to disturb the creatures in the coldest months. Throughout the spring the children have the opportunity to watch the tadpoles changing and see the plants return to the water. These frequent visits have helped the children to remember the safety rules and we rarely have any concerns whilst we use this area.

On this occasion, the children were hoping to find the frogs that would have hatched from the frogspawn they found earlier in the year. There followed a long conversation about where frogs would be and which places would be the best to look. A few of the children thought they would still be in the pond and went with an adult to look and the rest wanted to look in the plants around the pond.

One boy was able to tell me that the frogs would like damp places so they wouldn't be anywhere sunny. The children busied themselves looking in every corner. After a few minutes one child returned and told me that the frog might have gone back inside his eggs for a sleep.

Later that day, back in the setting, we shared a story about the life cycle of a frog. This same child then told me that the frog couldn't go back in his egg, but instead he would have gone to his friend's house! His friend's house was apparently quite cold and wet and the frog liked it there! I considered this a successful intervention to sort out a misconception!

12 August

Review of the year

For many of us this is the time of summer breaks and the opportunity to reflect on the previous year and to look forward to the next one. This time of evaluation is crucial to the success of the next academic year and you will need to be honest about your results.

There will be some aspects of your forest school experiences that went well and others that weren't so successful. Consider whether your future planning will incorporate the same sessions or whether they will be altered. You will need to consider your likely new cohort, their previous experiences and their attendance in your setting. As in all early years establishments, changing groups of children will alter the way you provide experiences, but if forest school is relatively new for you it may be prudent to use similar planning initially. By now you will be astute at tuning in to children's interests and will be more confident in allowing them to lead the play.

Your evaluation should include detail about health and safety: how effective are the risk assessments and how often are they monitored? Renew them in this quieter month, using feedback from other participants. Would you like to introduce something new in the coming year, for example: a rope swing or bridge? Carefully analyse the legal requirements that are required for your setting and the age group you are working with. Write new risk assessments and ensure they are effectively contributed to by your staff.

Have you considered asking your parents for their feedback? Perhaps they could complete a simple questionnaire, or maybe you would prefer to have a small core of parents in a forum session? Use their ideas to help you decide on your provision for the following year.

If your forest school takes place within a school, you will already have thought about how you will be supporting your new reception children and improving the transition for your older ones moving to Year 1.

Start to compile a list of essential jobs for the beginning of the autumn term. Consider resources, staffing, ratios, the environment, parent support and if you are prepared to use some of your summer holiday, you may find it helpful to map out an overview of forest school planning for the new term.

TO DO

- The forest school environment will still be in a time of rapid change and growth. Keep the social areas clear and make sure the majority of the paths do not become too overgrown.

- If this is a quiet month in your settings look at the semi-permanent structures and dens. Do they need some maintenance or even replacing?

- Carry out a resource audit. What will you need to replace or buy? Make a wish list and prioritise in your ordering.

- Sort through the resources boxes, putting everything back where it began and replacing damaged or missing items. If you still have children in your setting they will enjoy helping with this.
- Plan an overview of your autumn term provision, taking into account the age, group size and experience of your new cohort.

August at forest school

If you work in a nursery that runs throughout the year you may well find that your numbers are reduced as families take their summer holidays. Planning exciting experiences for the children that remain with you is important. There are several scenarios that you may have to contend with. There may be an influx of older children returning for holiday clubs, some of your experienced staff may be taking their breaks and some of the younger children are likely to be unsettled by the changes to their normal environment. In this instance forest school becomes a constant, familiar resource, which will help children to feel continuity and comfort. Modify and be flexible, but do your utmost to continue it throughout the month.

Keeping activities and resources familiar helps new children settle and regular visitors continue to be independent.

Staying safe in the sun

Objectives

- To understand how they can keep themselves safe from the sun.
- To utilise the available resources to create their own shade.

Adult initiated ideas

Provide the den building resource box – covers, rope, string etc. – and suggest the children may want to find a way of staying out of the heat of the day. Den building is likely to have been one of your staple activities throughout the year so it will be familiar to the children and should be an activity they can attempt on their own.

Provide some adult support to tie the den higher if the children want it be. They may be happy for it to be just high enough to crawl under.

Help the children make a simple tepee. Three or four sticks of similar length, tied at one end, and a piece of fabric is all that is needed for the children to have their own one or two person tent.

Do the children want to create seating inside? What can they use?

Leave the shelters up throughout the session and ask the children to share each other's ideas and use this to improve their own.

How else can the children keep themselves out of the sun? Look for shaded areas, provide hats and parasols.

Even on a cooler summer day these two girls benefited from a tarpaulin shelter.

Taking a break under the trees.

Making a home for a woodlouse

> **Objectives**
> - To look for and identify some mini-beasts.
> - To begin to know about the preferred habitats of mini-beasts.
> - To make a temporary home for woodlice.

Adult initiated ideas

Provide the mini-beast hunt kit. Ensure that it is complete with some simple identification charts, with pictures and simple words. Some of your cohort may be quite proficient early readers by now and will enjoy being able to read the words, 'spider', 'ladybird' and 'ant'.

Encourage the children to consider the specific places they are looking at. Is it damp, wet, dry, shady etc.? Can they record their findings on a simple record sheet or map that shows each bug and its location?

Perhaps the children could make small flags to push into the ground near the mini-beast's location? Draw a picture of the find on the flag so that other children will know what to look for.

If you have a nettle patch you are likely to find ladybirds in abundance. Remind children to be cautious of stinging plants.

Please remember to return all finds to their original hiding place.

Back at the setting provide a selection of junk, some soil, leaves, stones and sticks and encourage the children to make a new home for a woodlouse. Should it be dark or light, dry or damp?

Looking for woodlice involves finding some damp places in the sun-dried grounds.

What is it like to be a mini-beast?

Objectives

- To use their knowledge of where mini-beasts live to make their own related observations about the forest school area.
- To recognise some of the physical differences in different areas of the forest school site.
- To make observations about their own self in each of these specific areas.

Adult initiated ideas

Remind the children about their mini-beast hunt in the previous session and recap some of the language they used: dry, damp, cool, warm etc.

Can the children find areas that make them feel some of these things? Identify the spaces that are cooler, shadier, damper than others. Does the area feel the same as the drier places? Talk about the undergrowth, the soil, the tree bark and low-level plants. It is likely that the damp areas will be mossy, the bark may be greener. The plants growing may be different: can the children find something growing in a damp place that is not elsewhere?

How do the children feel in each of the areas? Encourage them to think about how mini-beasts might feel under their stones or hiding under a log.

Help the children set up two contrasting camp areas for their play and observations. Which one do they prefer and why?

If the camps remain for a few sessions children's reactions may be different according to the weather on the days they visit.

Whilst looking for woodlice these children discovered that ladybirds seemed to like the nettle patch.

The children were excited to find a small newt on their woodlice hunt.

Exploring the power of the sun

> ### Objectives
>
> - To use the heat of the sun to explore their world.
> - To explore their environment comparing the insects they find with those found in other sessions.

Adult initiated ideas

Provide a variety of water containers and brushes and encourage the children to use them for water painting. They can paint the ground, the fences, the shed door, the tree trunks – in fact anywhere!

Encourage children to think about what will happen to their painting when the sun is shining on it.

Look for some flowers that enjoy the sunny spots and talk about the flower parts. Identify the flower face and note which way it is facing; perhaps take a photo to help make comparisons later. Are all the flowers facing the same way?

Many flowers track the sun. Can the children think why they might do that? In simple terms the flowers that are facing the sun are warming up and therefore attract more insects to pollinate them. Are there any bees or insects that are enjoying the flowers?

Sunflowers are especially good at tracking the sun, so perhaps with some forward planning you could plant some to watch when they bloom?

If you have a wild-flower meadow use the warmest days to explore the insects that are using it. Are they the same as those the children found in the darker, damper places?

Provide paper and paints for the children to draw what they see. Introduce the idea of folding a painted picture to make their butterflies symmetrical. Hang the paintings on the washing line to dry in the sun.

The children used a bucket of water and some paintbrushes to make paintings on the playground.

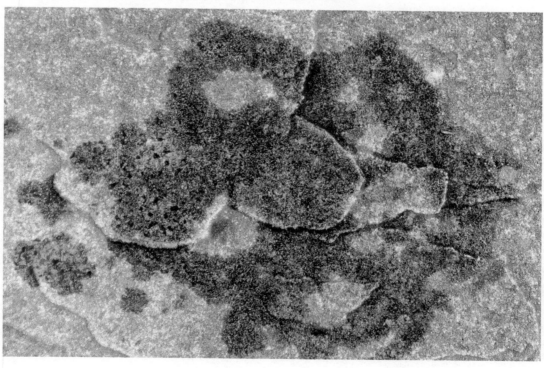

Child initiated ideas

What you provide for the children throughout this month will depend greatly on the age range with which you are working. If your cohort and forest school group has remained the same they will enjoy planning their play with you and their ideas and resources can be easily incorporated into your session. If your group includes some additional, less confident children you will need to help them settle in with familiar items around them.

I would suggest that you provide plenty of resources that allow for children to follow their interests unrestricted by cold and wet weather and with the bonus of green, dense undergrowth and tree cover. Take advantage of these natural assets and allow the children a chance to explore them freely, within your forest school rules of course.

RESOURCES

Adult initiated ideas:

- Forest school kit bag
- Forest school drinks bag
- Den building resource box
- Sun hats and parasols
- Mini-beast hunt kit
- Flag making resources: lolly sticks, sticky-tape, paper and pens
- Junk boxes, soil, stones, leaves, sticks
- Water containers, various sized brushes
- Paper, clipboard, watercolour paint sets and brushes

Child initiated idea:

- Create this resource list with the children, allow them to choose freely

Case study

Billy is a confident four-year-old boy, familiar with using forest school, and a regular attender in the setting. He was full of confidence and was always completely sure of what he wanted to do whilst he was at forest school.

During August he was rather unsettled and was clearly missing his friends who had finished for the summer and whom he would join up with when he started school the following month. He became a little clingy and began having some separation issues. Aware that the most likely reason was his missing friends the staff went to a great deal of trouble to make him feel more secure. In the setting he was asked to help with the younger children, put in charge of getting out specific toys and clearing them away. He relished this new role and enjoyed having a task to do as he arrived.

On his weekly visit to forest school Billy continued in his supporting role, taking charge of one of the younger children, showing them his favourite places and helping them find games to play.

It was Billy who asked if he could choose the boxes and baskets they had to play with on his visit and he helped a member of staff select and carry the resources to the area.

The unsettled time quickly passed for Billy due to the alertness of his key-worker and he enjoyed the rest of his summer as one of the 'grown ups'. He frequently made suggestions about what he felt the younger children would enjoy and made reference to some of the things he had done on his first few visits. At the end of his forest school session, he was already talking about what he wanted to do on his next visit.

Monthly blog

After a particularly sunny afternoon enjoying the forest school area and the wild flowers, a group of girls were overheard discussing the flowers that faced the sun. It transpired that they wanted to know if all flowers faced the sun.

With some careful questioning we were able to lead them towards finding out for themselves. The three girls agreed they would go outside in the garden and look at the flowers; if they were facing the sun the girls would put a brick beside them and come back and tell us. It took them some time to explore the garden and when I was taken back out there were little collections of bricks scattered among the daisies on the grass.

The girls were excited to tell me that the daisies were all 'looking at the sky'.

They told me the daisies were 'looking for a bug to live in them' and that when they had found the bug they would close and keep it inside them.

I prompted the girls to lie quietly and still waiting for a bug to come along. In the relatively short wait one of the girls wandered off but the others remained. Eventually they called out there was a bug 'going to live in the daisy'.

I went to watch and encouraged the girls to stay and see whether the daisy closed. After a couple of minutes the bug flew off and the daisy remained open. One of the girls told me that the bug hadn't liked that flower and was going to find a new one. It turned out that the girl and her family had been viewing new houses!

Finding flowers that turn to face the sun.

Conclusion

This book came about through a desire to share my experience, to reinforce my beliefs and extend the outdoor learning movement into more places and settings. I hope that within it you have found a manageable way of using forest school in your everyday practice.

This year, more than any other, the children in my class had a full and busy time in the outdoor classroom. Our focus is always to increase independence and provide new opportunities, but this year, with the focus of this publication at the fore, my planning was more detailed, linked securely to indoor experiences and closely related to the children's own styles and modes of learning.

These children, leaving my class at the end of the academic year, have grown in confidence and independence more than any other group I have worked with. They have found their own play, explored freely, tried new experiences and shared openly with others. We have worked with the on-site pre-school, preparing them for their year of forest school and worked hard with the parents to develop our work space further. We have developed our planting scheme, re-made our log circle, used the plastic bottle greenhouse effectively and successfully brought the outside learning back to the classroom. These children are happy and able learners, ready to move through their education with confidence and enthusiasm.

Showing satisfaction at having completed his task.

Having the confidence to choose their own learning opportunities.

Sharing their findings with their friends.

The benefits of our experiences are hard to measure on paper, but in self-esteem and contentment they are obvious to all involved.

We have dealt with extreme weather conditions and at a time when much of Somerset suffered with severe floods we used this in our learning: floating boats, watching the rings on the water and mixing mud pies. We didn't have the extreme cold of previous years, so we replicated it with a freezer to make the ice instead. We've had to be creative in our approach, we've learnt more about the children than we could have imagined and understand learning styles in a more complex way.

Sharing experiences with children from other year groups.

Recording their findings has become a regular experience for these children.

We have inspired the teaching in other year groups and enjoyed the involvement of all the children regardless of their age and year group. By closely monitoring, observing and talking we have given the children in our care the best opportunities in their earliest years. The long-term success is hard to measure, but I fully believe that these children have an affinity with their world that would otherwise have been missing.

One of the hardest things about putting together a collection of activities for forest school is my belief that much of forest school needs to be led by the children. The very nature of putting a session or activity in writing takes away this principle before we have even got outside. But however contradictory I now sound, it really is an essential requirement for the long-term success of your adventure into the outdoors.

I don't doubt that faced with a wide open, tree covered space children will always find a way to occupy themselves and will create their own learning opportunities. But will all children? In my experience there are always a few children who don't have the confidence to climb into hedges, roll logs around or catch mini-beasts. It is these children that need some structure initially, even if just for a week or two, before they take off to explore freely. It is your role as a forest school practitioner to show the children how they can use their environment to learn and explore. Given a wide variety of activities to explore will inspire the children to develop their own ideas further, and almost always in a way that you could not have planned for.

Planning serves several purposes: it ensures you have the right resources and the correct staffing; it helps you maintain the learning experiences that have been inspired inside the classroom; it provides evidence of the delivery of a broad curriculum and allows you to make the necessary observations and assessment. Sadly, as we all know, justifying what we do with our children all day also plays a crucial role in the wider school environment and showing how we meet the needs of these children is entirely necessary. Planning can show all this.

Working together to explore their outdoor environment these children have extended their own learning experiences.

But more important than the planning is the evaluation of what actually took place; it will usually be different to your initial thoughts and unexpected from the planned outcomes. Making note of how the children learned allows you to ensure that future experiences are tailored to these needs. This evaluation will also highlight how secure and confident your children are becoming, whether they are independent doers and thinkers, how their friendships are developing and whether they are able to work with their friends.

So while this book is a sample of planned experiences and opportunities, it is also a demonstration of fluid, child-led experiences. So by all means follow the plans, set up the resources and provide those experiences, but watch what the children are really doing, adapt the opportunities and make note of the learning that actually takes place.

I hope that throughout the book I have been honest about how the children have taken the learning in their own direction and how even the most well prepared sessions have fallen foul to the weather conditions.

I have been leading forest school for almost twenty years and I still set out with a plan, a pile of resources and some high expectations. But I am still surprised at the outcomes, amazed at the intuition of the children and excited by the learning.

I hope that you find the same fulfilment in your role and that the children you care for learn about their environment, about their abilities and about themselves on their way to becoming well-rounded, secure and happy young people.

> Give children as much autonomy as you can. Allow them to take risks. Let them get dirty! They need to work out the rules of the world and boundaries, without you taking over.
> Dr David Whitebread, Senior Lecturer in Psychology of Education
> University of Cambridge
> *The Daily Telegraph*, 17 February 2014

Treat the outdoors as your classroom without walls and your children will be rewarded with opportunities that exceed all your expectations.

Useful books to share and inspire the children

Boyd, M. (2013) *The RSPB Children's Guide to Nature Watching.* London: A & C Black Children's and Educational.

Carle, E. (1969) *The Very Hungry Caterpillar.* London: Hamish Hamilton.

Carle, E. (1997) *The Tiny Seed.* London: Puffin Books.

Donaldson, J. (1999) *The Gruffalo.* London: Macmillan Children's Books.

Green, S. (2011) *Outdoor Explorers.* London: Franklin Watts.

Howe, A. (2005) *Play Using Natural Materials.* London: David Fulton Publishers.

Parker, S. and Goodman, P. (2002) *Artyfacts. Minibeasts.* London: Abbey Children's Books.

Rosen, M. (1997) *We're Going on a Bear Hunt.* London: Walker Books Ltd.

Schofield, J. and Danks, F. (2012) *The Stick Book: Loads of Things You Can Do With a Stick.* London: Frances Lincoln Ltd.

Ward, J. (2008) *I Love Dirt: 52 Activities to Help You and Your Kids Discover the Wonders of Nature.* Boston and London: Trumpeter.

Useful reading

Bilton, H. (1999) *Outdoor Play in the Early Years: Management and Improvement*. London: David Fulton Publishers.

Bradford, H. (2012) *Planning and Observation of Children under Three*. London and New York: Routledge.

Constable, K. (2012) *The Outdoor Classroom, Ages 3–7: Using Ideas from Forest Schools to Enrich Learning*. London and New York: Routledge.

Constable, K. (2013) *Planning for Schematic Learning in the Early Years: A Practical Guide*. London and New York: Routledge.

DfES (2006) *Learning Outside the Classroom Manifesto*. Nottingham: Crown Publications.

Doyle, J. and Milchem, K. (2012) *Developing an Early Years Forest School*. London: Practical Pre-School Books.

Early Years Foundation Stage Profile Handbook (2013) Crown Copyright.

Ephgrave, A. (2011) *The Reception Year in Action: A Month-by-Month Guide to Success in the Classroom*. London and New York: Routledge.

Fisher, J. (1996) *Starting from the Child*. Buckingham: Open University Press.

Green, J. (2010) *Learning Outside the Classroom: Early Years and Key Stage 1*. Leamington Spa: LCP.

Green, S. (2009) *Protection, Safety and Welfare in the Early Years*. Practical Pre-School. London: Step Forward Publishing.

Green, S. (2011) *Outdoor Explorers*. London: Franklin Watts.

Harriman, H. (2006) *The Outdoor Classroom: A Place to Learn*. Swindon: Corner to Learn.

Isaacs, B. (2010) *Bringing the Montessori Approach to your Early Years Practice, 2nd Edition*. London and New York: Routledge.

Knight, S. (2009) *Forest Schools and Outdoor Learning in the Early Years*. London: Sage Publications.

Lindon, J. (1999) *Too Safe For Their Good*. London: The National Early Years Network.

Louv, R. (2005) *Last Child in the Woods: Saving our Children from Nature Deficit Disorder*. London: Atlantic Books.

Nicol, J. (2010) *Bringing the Waldorf Steiner Approach to Early Years, 2nd Edition*. London and New York: Routledge.

O'Brien, E. and Murray, R. (2006) *A Marvellous Opportunity for Children to Learn: A Participatory Evaluation of Forest School in England and Wales*. Farnham: Forest Research.

Rodger, R. (1999) *Planning and Appropriate Curriculum for the Under Fives*. London: David Fulton Publishers.

Ryder Richardson, G. (2006) *Creating a Space to Grow: Developing your Outdoor Learning Environment*. London: David Fulton Publishers.

Thornton, L. and Brunton, P. (2010) *Bringing the Reggio Approach to your Early Years Practice, 2nd Edition*. London and New York: Routledge.

Tovey, H. (2007) *Playing Outdoors: Spaces and Places, Risk and Challenge*. Maidenhead: Open University Press.

Tovey, H. (2013) *Bringing the Froebel Approach to your Early Years Practice, 2nd Edition*. London and New York: Routledge.

Warden, C. (2010) *Nature Kindergartens*. Scotland: Mindstretchers.

Watts, A. (2013) *Outdoor Learning through the Seasons: An Essential Guide for the Early Years.* London and New York: Routledge.